Assessing PNDL

Anca Monica Marin

Assessing PNDL

Romanian Leaders in Quest for State-Budget Funds

Springer

Anca Monica Marin
Research Institute for Quality of Life
Romanian Academy
Bucharest, Romania

ISBN 978-3-030-82843-1 ISBN 978-3-030-82844-8 (eBook)
https://doi.org/10.1007/978-3-030-82844-8

This Springer imprint is published by the registered company Springer Nature Switzerland AG
The registered company address is: Gewerbestrasse 11, 6330 Cham, Switzerland

Preface

This book might seem at first glance as a focused one-case example of a state budget program from a former post-communist country. Yet, I hope it's more than that. I wanted to bring as much objectiveness as possible to a case which seemed to be best-known though never thoroughly "proved" as a case of political influence over the distribution of funds. I also wanted to use the available open data as a way to show that self-funded research is still possible (although not always the best path to follow). It's also a way to explore and combine various open data sources, so as to add comprehensiveness in the analysis.

I have been involved in projects concerning local and central authorities in Romania for almost 20 years. They cover a lot of the hot topics corresponding to different periods in time, such as decentralization, accession in the EU, EU funds absorption, and administrative capacity. I collaborated with many experts, from which I learned a lot, and I am really thankful for the numerous working opportunities. The problem of political influence has been a recurrent topic throughout all of the above. And it surely is an important topic. Nevertheless, I wanted to add a larger perspective and magnify the lens through which I am looking at state budget funds through a comparison with EU funds. As this was the topic of my PhD dissertation, I assumed it will play a significant part in my analysis. I wish that the way to look at data as they are presented in this book is an instrument for decision makers to better coordinate their decisions. Yet, up to the present time, they did not seem to do so. Maybe the new programming period for EU funds will be a good place to start.

Adding on, I am living in a country where allocations for research and development are constantly among the lowest in the EU. I am working at the intersection of multiple fields of knowledge (sociology, public finance, public administration), which still seem, in the eyes of various politicians and bureaucrats, to produce nothing relevant as research products. Perhaps it's time to change their minds. Education, research, and development are there to serve their decisions and constructively criticize them, if the case occurs.

Lastly, this is a self-funded book and my family significantly supported its accomplishment. Nonetheless, my family supported me throughout the years, from university to the present time, in all the large or small-scale projects I have been working. My parents and my brother, and later on my husband and my daughter, continually encouraged and trusted me. My deepest gratitude goes to them. I realize I have been and continue to be very lucky because of them.

Bucharest, Romania Anca Monica Marin

Acknowledgments

This is a self-funded book. It could not have been finalized without the constant support from my family. Special thanks go to my mother, husband, and daughter. Their questions on the book's topic and the use of sociology in general proved to act as a source of support for me to be able to improve the study. My daughter was the light at the end of the tunnel during the writing of this book, which seemed to be endless. I also kept in mind all the time the encouragement and trust from my late father.

I would also like to thank my colleagues at ICCV and CERME. Working in projects with them in teams led by Manuela Sofia Stănculescu opened up new research horizons for me. They helped me enact the same research rigor and quality standards I have been used to in working with them.

Another thank you goes to Alin Chis, who helped me create the maps at a national level based on the data computations I have made for this book.

Last but not least, I would like to thank participants in the qualitative research, representatives of mayoralties, and county councils. They kindly accepted to talk to me on the topic of PNDL II while the entire country was under a state of alert as a consequence of the COVID-19 pandemic. Their insights on the topic helped in refining the interpretation of results.

Contents

Acronyms

ANCPI	National Agency for Cadastre and Land Register
CC	County Council
CERME	Romanian Centre for Economic Modelling
CNI	National Company of Investments
CPF	County Partnership Framework
DG	General Directorate
EU	European Union
EFOR	Expert Forum
GEO	Governmental Emergency Ordinance
GD	Government Decision
ICCV	Research Institute for Quality of Life
LAG	Local Action Group
LG	Local Government
MDRAP	Ministry of Regional Development and Public Administration
MDRAPFE	Ministry of Regional Development, Public Administration and European Funds (former MDRAP)
MFP	Ministry of Public Finances
MLDPA	Ministry of Public Works, Development and Administration (former MDRAP)
MP	Member of the Parliament
POIM	Operational Program for Large Infrastructure
POR	Regional Operational Program
PNDL	National Program for Local Development
PNDL I	First Session of PNDL (2013–2020)
PNDL II	Second Session of PNDL (2017–2020)
PNDR	National Plan for Rural Development
PNCIPS	National Program for Investments in Buildings of Public or Social Interest
PSD	Social Democratic Party
PNL	National Liberal Party
RAS	Reimbursable Advisory Services

SIRUTA	Informatics System of the Registry of Administrative-Territorial Units
UDMR	Democratic Alliance of Hungarians in Romania
WB	World Bank

List of Figures

List of Tables

Chapter 1
Rationale

1.1 What Is this Book About

This book is about the predictors of getting funds from Romania's largest State Budget funded program—National Program for Local Development (PNDL). It aims to contribute to an objective assessment of the way State Budget funds from Romania's largest program are allocated at the level of county councils and municipalities in the urban and rural area.

Most of the debate around this program have been carried out more in the circle of politicians and less in that of scientific research. This study aims to fill in this gap by bringing in the spotlight a national-level analysis on this topic, based on a secondary analysis of publicly available data.

One more argument in favour of this book: it has been self-funded. This means, on the one hand, it took a much longer time than expected to complete it, but, on the other hand, there has been no external influence on the researcher. This signifies that the book is a purely independent project, which seeks to add both global as well as detailed view on this issue.

1.2 Why Reading this Book

Potential readers of this book include researchers, politicians, civil servants, consultants, decision-makers. Nonetheless, this does not yet answer why reading this book.

First, it might seem another (boring) study on public administration, politicisation, regional and county-level development imbalances, etc. You might as well consider all of these still true by the end of the book. Yet, in my experience, 'following the money' is always an interesting topic. The theoretical approach combines concepts and approaches from the fields of sociology, public management and public finance. Numbers and statistical analyses might prove boring, but when

A. M. Marin, *Assessing PNDL*, https://doi.org/10.1007/978-3-030-82844-8_1

comparing sources of funding (like PNDL and European funds) for the same territorial administrative unit—for instance, the county council—it might yield a whole different picture. This is why stakeholders acting in the field of EU funds might also be interested in this book, although the title suggests that we are only looking at State Budget funds.

Secondly, this study introduces new predictors tested in the model of statistical analyses, at least in the case of Romania. One such example is the length of tenure of the president of the County Council. It has been named as 'experience of the President of the County Council'. The public media uses the president of the County Council (party affiliation, tenure length, overall influence in the political party) as a self-explanatory factor. Still, now we test, at least partially, its influence in a statistical model of multiple regression. It means that all other independent variables included in the model are held constant.

Thirdly, it adds another lens to look at the funded investments—investments in the areas where these capital expenditures are highly needed: rural marginalised areas. The book has a dedicated sub-section on whether rural marginalised areas are also marginalised from allocation of PNDL funds. This means that specialists in local development, poverty and fiscal management might be interested in reading this book.

Last but not least, the book includes a section considering the relevance of studying PNDL in the current context of the global crisis of COVID-19 pandemic.

To sum up, the book is a plea for coordination of investments, policy priorities and, mostly, improved transparency of selection, funding and monitoring of investments at community-level, irrespective of the source of funding. The whole approach encompasses a theoretical lens which combines developments in the sociology of organisations and public administration to grasp the complex funding environment of first and second-tier level institutions in Romania.

1.3 Structure of the Book

The book is divided into eight sections. The first section adds further arguments to the ones listed above on why study Romania, PNDL and State Budget funded programs. The second one shows the study's methodology, including a presentation of data sources, together with research limitations. The third section presents the study context, with an overview of Romanian local public administration and the context of State Budget funded programs. The fourth section covers various concepts and approaches from sociology, public management and public finance towards confining a theoretical approach. The fifth section hands out results grouped around the three levels of analysis: the second tier of public administration—County Councils, and the first tier of public administration—urban and rural municipalities. The sixth section includes a section on updating the information on PNDL allocations at the level of the year 2020. The seventh section considers the relevance of studying PNDL in the context of COVID-19 pandemic. Conclusions and recommendations are provided in the last section of the book. They include a sub-section on what could (better) be done as further steps to this research.

1.4 Why Study Romania?

For Romanian researchers or foreign researchers interested in Romania, such as researchers from other post-communist countries, the title of this sub-section might seem a redundant topic. Yet, for a part of researchers from other geographical areas, including other EU countries, this prompts out as a recurrent question mark.

At first sight, the topic of funds' allocation from the State Budget funded program in Romania is a particular and specific topic, placed in one of the least developed countries in the EU. It thus adds knowledge on one country where intensive scientific research on this topic is still lagging behind.

Even so, this book is about more than that. It studies the issue of National Program for Local Development in a comprehensive manner with a conceptual framework at the crossroads of sociology, public management and public finance.

Romania's vertical and horizontal power imbalances might prove to be valid in other contexts too. This is why the section on study context presents an overview of Romanian local public administration and a closer look at the context of the State Budget funded programs. Where available, comparisons with other EU countries are included.

This study also covers a comparative overview of the volume of funds with EU funds allocation at the territorial administrative unit level (county or municipality). This topic is highly relevant for the EU funds programming process. A similar type of analysis could be conducted in the context of other EU local governments.

Last but not least, Romania is (still) part of the EU. Therefore, any study adding knowledge to Romania's situation is potentially adding knowledge in the European context as well.

1.5 Why Study State Budget Funded Programs and PNDL?

To put it simply, because they fund a large part of investments in Romania. In this respect, Romania still needs substantial investments in infrastructure, especially in rural and small urban areas.

There is a substantial need for critical investments in infrastructure projects in Romania. This need is not entirely matched by the available EU funds. WB's study from 2015 identified considerable funding gaps in key areas for investment funded by PNDL. These funding gaps are presented in Table 1.1. The remaining funding gap from Table 1.1 does not necessarily mean that there have not been other State Budget funded programs covering this funding gap. These are represented by previous allocations from PNDL, like PNDL 2015–2019, or subsequent allocations

Table 1.1 Investment needs vs. supply of EU funds (2014–2020) (euro)

Priority sector	Investment need	Proposed EU allocations for 2014–2020	Funding gap	PNDL allocations 2017–2020	Remaining funding gap (after PNDL II)
County roads	3,412,193,664	946,808,511	2,465,383,153	978,219,974	1,487,163,179
Communal roads	4,728,319,110	440,236,880	4,288,083,230	1,811,601,345	2,476,481,885
Water and wastewater	23,804,837,000	3,014,236,880	20,790,600,120	1,819,859,956	18,970,740,164
Social infrastructure	3,705,110,000	522,370,000	3,182,740,000	980,630,378	2,202,109,622
Total	35,650,459,774	4,923,652,271	30,726,807,503	5,590,311,653	25,136,495,850

Source: Burduja et al. (2015, 17) and author's calculations for PNDL allocations and remaining funding gap. Notes: Investment needs are calculated based on the World Bank methodology for each of these sectors. EU allocations are those proposed in the draft programming documents for the ROP, PNDR and OP Large Infrastructure. PNDL allocations 2017–2020 are computed based on a unique code assigned for each investment, based on the official data for the stage of implementation as of May 1, 2018. The sum allocated for communal roads is based on street infrastructure investments in the rural municipalities. Investments for bridges are not included in the sum allocated for county or communal roads. The sums allocated for social infrastructure include investments for high school/schools/ inclusive education/ kindergartens/ health infrastructures. All the sums allocated from PNDL 2017–2020 are transformed in euro, based on an annual average exchange rate published by the National Bank of Romania

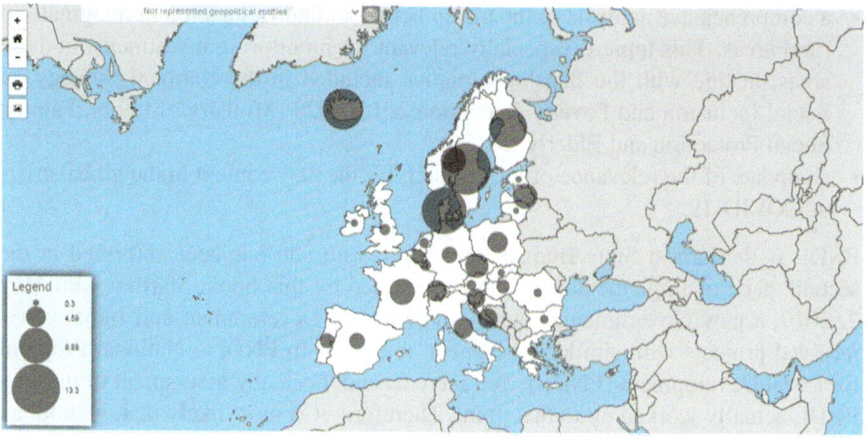

Fig. 1.1 Distribution in the EU of Main national accounts tax aggregates—Local Government, 2018 (% of GDP). Source: Eurostat, https://ec.europa.eu/eurostat/databrowser/view/GOV_10A_TAXAG__custom_11630/default/map?lang=en (date of access: September 28, 2020)

from PNDL 2017–2020, not included in the present analysis.[1] Nevertheless, the table shows that the funding objectives included in PNDL 2017–2020 address critical needs in Romanian infrastructure. Additionally, investment expenditures have constantly been lower than the projected ones, including EU funds (Fiscal Council, 2019, 6). Consequently, their transparent and efficient distribution is of utmost importance for ensuring a significant contribution to an increased quality of life in urban and rural areas. In addition to the investment needs presented in Table 1.1, the allocations from PNDL II also cover investments in county/ urban/ rural bridges, public street lighting systems and public institutions offices.

Furthermore, the context of a local government with low financial autonomy (Fig. 1.1) and highly needing infrastructure update brings about additional opportunities for studying, for instance, the influence of the mayor's political affiliation in funds allocation. Yet, this topic is not the field of anecdotal evidence, but the subject of sound statistical analysis.

Additionally, the book brings about several other lenses to magnify the view:

- a comparative overview of the volume of funds with EU funds allocation at the territorial administrative unit level (county or municipality). This topic is highly applicable to the EU funds programming process;
- a detailed analysis of investment objectives at county, urban and rural municipality levels;

[1] The current analysis covers the allocations from PNDL published as of May 1, 2018, available here: http://www.mdrap.ro/lucrari-publice/pndl. The sixth section includes an update of the information at the level of the year 2020.

- a comprehensive analysis of the match between funds allocation in marginalised rural areas. This topic is especially relevant for monitoring investments in these areas, in line with the flagship initiative included in the National Strategy on Social Inclusion and Poverty Reduction 2015–2020 (Ministry of Labor, Family, Social Protection and Elderly, 2015).
- an update of the relevance of the research for the new context in the global crisis of COVID-19.

PNDL is the largest State Budget funded program and has been reformed in the second stage of implementation, the one studied by this book. Starting with May 2, 2019, a new Governmental Fund—the Fund of Development and Initiatives—received projects with similar investment objectives to PNDL—National Program for Local Development (PNDL). Yet, there has not been any assessment of the way PNDL actually worked up to that point. Therefore, it is most likely that, without an objective assessment, any new similar Fund will only maintain deficiencies in the allocation mechanisms.

Previous studies state there is a subjective allocation of funds for the local government in Romania (Thijs et al., 2018a) including the programs managed by the Ministry analysed in this paper—Ministry of Regional Development and Public Administration: 'In general, counties with the same political make-up as the central government receive more funds. This procedure can lead to funding amounting to 5–20% of the county budget coming from the central government for special projects. This kind of examples includes counties such as Cluj or Tulcea, which were supported by the centre-right coalitions and Teleorman and Constanţa which were supported by centre-left coalitions' (Thijs et al., 2018a, 851). Yet, there is no clear or specific evidence provided in support of this argument. This paper is an objective analysis based on empirical data of the distribution of funds for a specific program targeting local government in Romania. This is actually the only way to understand public administration characteristics in a specific country. The value-added of this book is making a step further in using only 'experts-opinions' as is the case with other various indicators on public administration.

Many challenges outlined in the WB's report on coordinating EU and State Budget funded programs in Romania (Burduja et al., 2015) still remain true nowadays:

- There is a poor design of large State Budget funded programs like PNDL, and there is no systematic effort to coordinate interventions in public investments. It is worth mentioning that the term coordination is used in regard to both vertical coordination (across administrative levels) as well as horizontal coordination (across sectors and/or across jurisdictions) (Burduja et al., 2015, 3). Under this topic, improvements have been made based on WB's policy recommendations. Yet, the long history of weak vertical and horizontal coordination in Romanian public administration provides much room for improvement even at present time. This study compares the volume of funds absorbed on the one hand, in the previous programming period for EU funds and on the other hand, the one absorbed through PNDL 2017–2020. It also provides an analysis of disparities across administrative levels (county councils/ municipalities) as well as urban-rural municipalities. Finally, it adds insights from the qualitative and the desk research conducted for the purpose of this study.

- The prioritisation criteria are considered vague, subjective and opaque, and project selection much less rigorous than under EU structural funds (Burduja et al., 2015, 5). Yet, there has been substantial improvement with PNDL II based on the work performed by WB (Marteau et al., 2014; Burduja et al., 2015). I would add that this does not mean that project selection under EU structural funds has been rigorously made in all cases. Previous studies (Marin, 2015) identify significant challenges in many areas, including EU funded public investments, similar to PNDL investments. In addition, political affiliation and the mayor's social capital play their roles in 'selection' of EU funding winners.
- Monitoring and evaluation mechanisms for state-funded programs are rudimentary. In this respect, this work's methodology and approach significantly contribute to an intermediary evaluation of the improved version of PNDL, PNDL II (2017–2020), limited to the data allocation officially published as of May 1, 2018. Almost all indicators used in the analysis can be included in an institutional monitoring and evaluation mechanism to track the progress of the program. The current presentations of the program's stages of implementation[2] provide only basic data, aggregated either at county or national level, or by investment objectives.
- 'On top of everything, the overall environment in Romania is not particularly conducive to coordination, for a myriad of reasons' (Burduja et al., 2015, 6). One of the reasons identified by WB's study is the lack of a solid history of collaboration among public institutions. Most likely, this has also to do with the interplay between local public finances management and the power relationships across administrative levels, especially between the county councils and rural municipalities.
- The recent WB's Country Partnership Framework (CPF, 2018) states that all projects selected under the PNDL program since 2016 are assessed using a new set of selection criteria (approved by Ministerial Order 947/2015). As a result, all public investment projects are selected based on improved evaluation and selection criteria under PNDL. Nevertheless, the same document states that: "Through the regional development RAS program, the Bank provided recommendations on prioritization of investments, introducing multiyear budgeting, budgeting by program and proposed selection criteria options; the client (MDRAP) has adopted all our recommendations except for the selection criteria which only partially followed the Bank's recommendations" (World Bank, 2018a: 65–66). Therefore, it might be useful to examine the results of the mix of allocation criteria based on MDRAP internal decisions and WB's recommendations.

[2]Available here: http://www.mdrap.ro/lucrari-publice/pndl (date of access: February 13, 2019).

Furthermore, a performance analysis conducted for PNDL 2013–2014 implementation period (Romanian Court of Accounts, 2015) reveals several issues, amongst which:

(i) MDRAP has not conducted analyses based on prioritisation criteria, whenever supplementing or redistributing the initially allocated sums;
(ii) new objective investments have been funded in 2013 and 2014, although initially, the approval for funding was only for the current investment objectives, including the ones taken over by PNDL from other programs;
(iii) new objective investments have been approved for funding through Ministerial Orders in December, with only a few days term of validity;
(iv) MDRAP has not correlated the fields eligible for funding under PNDL and the National Program for Public or Social Interest Buildings, run by the National Company for Investments;
(v) part of the ministerial orders allocating funds for specific investment objectives have been followed after a long period by the corresponding funding contracts (longer than 30 days);
(vi) MDRAP has not efficiently monitored the implementation of funding contracts;
(vii) MDRAP has not ceased the contracts for those beneficiaries who did not comply with their responsibilities under the funding contracts.

Under this general context, the study provides a solid ground for substantiating the coordination of interventions in order to maximise the value-added of EU funds available in Romania.

Chapter 2
Methodology

2.1 Data and Method

This book relies on a triangulation of data sources and methods to increase the robustness of findings and conclusions. Findings based on a secondary analysis of open data have been put in the larger settings of the Romanian system of public administration, as a result of the extensive desk review and contextual analysis conducted. The desk research has also identified previous findings on similar topics/approaches. In addition, open data on PNDL II funding allocations published by the Ministry of Regional Development and Public Administration have been supplemented with relevant statistical information at locality level from the National Institute of Statistics, as well as local development indexes currently available—for rural localities, technical and building endowment index, as computed in a study by the Economic Studies Academy, index of local human development, as computed by professor Dumitru Sandu, together with various indicators (mainly on own revenues and EU funds) from the database of local budgets execution as published by a different department from the same ministry mentioned above—General Directorate of Public Administration, Directorate for Local Fiscal and Budgetary Policies. Based on the desk review, additional data sources have been integrated into a common database. They refer to data on the political affiliation of mayors' and President of the County Council from the local elections of 2016 as published by the Central Electoral Office and data on urban and rural municipalities which are part of a Local Action Group. All these quantitative data have been aggregated by the author in a common database at locality level. Furthermore, data from the budgetary allocations of PNDL II have been, on the one hand, integrated into a large database compiled at investment objective level and, on the other hand, aggregated at locality level, as a sum of all contracted investment objectives.

Another data compilation has been conducted for the entire dataset of projects in order to identify the most disaggregated level—village level. In total, 5379 projects have been analysed case-by-case in order to identify the village. This analysis has been performed in order to determine project localisation in respect to rural

A. M. Marin, *Assessing PNDL*, https://doi.org/10.1007/978-3-030-82844-8_2

marginalised areas. It has also been used to see whether the information published by MDRAP is sufficient to ascertain a specific localisation of the project. Precise project localisation is notably important for achieving coordination of investments at a national level.

Additionally, the quantitative analyses performed on the compiled databases have been complemented with the qualitative information collected through interviews conducted between December 2019–July 2020. The interviews have been conducted by phone, mainly due to the budgetary constraints for conducting this research project as well as within the context of COVID-19 pandemic. The key topics included in the interview guide have been focused on the process of funds' allocation, main bottlenecks and issues encountered, support received, specific recommendations for improving program management. Interviewed stakeholders included representatives of two county councils (three representatives, chiefs of departments/services), representatives of eight rural municipalities (mayors and local secretaries), as well as representatives of one urban settlement. In total, representatives of eleven public institutions from county, urban and rural levels expressed their opinions. Stakeholders participating in the qualitative research represented local communities placed in different development regions of Romania. They also included cases of municipalities with maximum and minimum allocations from PNDL II. In order to complement the information from the sources mentioned above, the author of the book also submitted requests of public information to the corresponding authority, the Ministry of Regional Development and Public Administration. These public information requests have been drafted and submitted to the Ministry by e-mail in October 2018, in line with the legislative framework on transparency of public information in Romania—Law no. 544/2001. Full texts of the public information requests[1] are available in the Annexes. Ministry's responses are included in the main text of the book as well as in the Annexes.

2.2 Data Sources

This book represents an exercise to use extensively open data published by Romanian public authorities. The key sources in this respect have been MDRAP (Ministry of Regional Development and Public Administration) for PNDL II allocations and MFP (Ministry of Public Finances) for local budgets execution (including information on European funds absorbed). In addition to allocations at locality level, there have also been public information requests submitted to the responsible Ministry—Ministry of Regional Development and Public Administration (Fig. 2.1). In order to test various predictors in a comprehensibly theoretical model, the study also uses data from:

[1]The public information requests have been drafted by the author and submitted as part of an institutional setting—Romanian Centre for Economic Modelling.

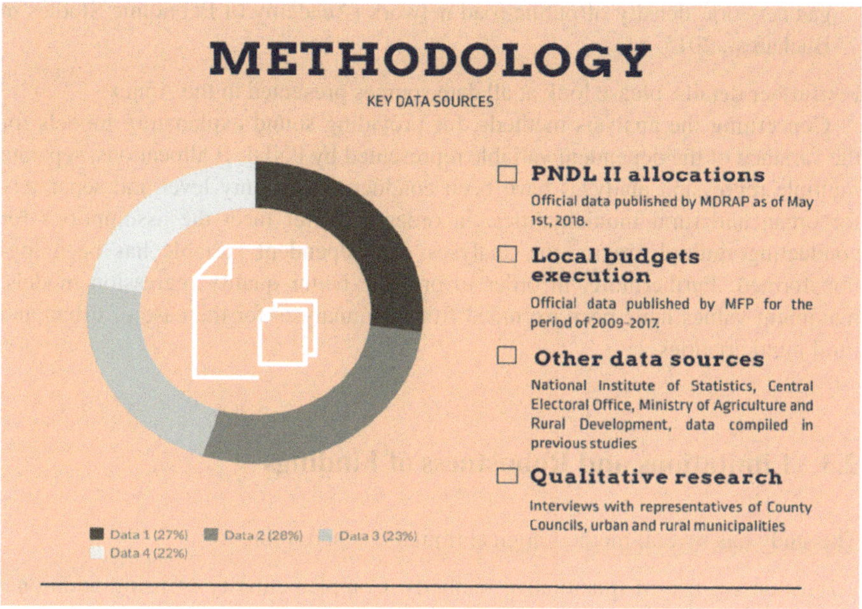

Fig. 2.1 Key data sources (Part of the figures from this book is created with the support of piktochart.com.)

- National Institute of Statistics—data on population from Census results, information on the length of modernised roads at county level, information on the total length of the simple network of drinking water distribution (data at locality level);
- Central Electoral Office—data on political party affiliation of the President of the County Council and of Mayor's;
- County Councils' websites—data on the experience of County Council's President (length of tenure more than 10 years long)
- Ministry of Agriculture and Rural Development—List of selected Local Action Groups, as of January 2019
- Index of locality development as processed by previous studies, namely Local Human Development Index as processed by professor Dumitru Sandu and an index on technical and building endowment of the rural municipalities, as processed by the Economic Studies Academy. Furthermore, data on rural marginalised areas at village level have been used based on a WB study—The Atlas of Rural Marginalized Areas and of Local Human Development in Romania (Teşliuc et al., 2016). The index of rural local infrastructure development has been used as computed by previous studies (Academy of Economic Studies in Bucharest, 2015). It includes information on the technical endowment at local level, including share of dwellings connected to water from the public network, share of dwellings connected to sewerage, share of dwellings connected to the

gas network, density of public road network (Academy of Economic Studies in Bucharest, 2015, 81).

For further details, please look at all data sources presented in the Annex.

Concerning the analysis methods, for providing sound explanatory models for the variance of the dependent variable represented by PNDL II allocations, separate multiple regression analyses have been conducted at county level and separately for urban and rural municipalities. In order to better meet the assumptions for conducting multiple regression analyses, the dependent variable has been log-transformed. Furthermore, in order to produce better quality regression models, maximum values have been excluded from the analysis for the case of urban and rural municipalities.

2.3 Limitations and Robustness of Findings

The study has several methodological limitations pertaining to:

(i) extensive use of quantitative methods. Complementarity of using additional qualitative information collected at county and locality level has been very useful, yet limited to a small number of interviews conducted by phone and marked by the pandemic crisis generated by COVID-19 context;
(ii) lack of public availability of data at the most disaggregated level[2] on the technical endowment of educational infrastructure, or on public lighting, technical conditions of mayoralties' offices. Nevertheless, it is not clear that at central level these data really exist at present time or existed in 2018,[3] centralised in the form of a searchable database. If they do exist, then the Ministry of Regional Development and Public Administration (or other responsible central public authorities) should make them public and use them as background data for elaborating public policies in their field, as well as for allocations at local level.
(iii) high variation of the dependent variable in case of rural municipalities. Although an explanatory model has been provided, it could be further improved by testing additional potentially significant predictors, depending on the available information at territorial administrative unit level.

Still, the quantitative analyses have been performed on a large number of municipalities and have been stratified across administrative levels. This fact together with multiple regression analyses adds notable robustness of findings. The provided explanatory models can only be improved if additional relevant information is collected/provided in a sufficiently disaggregated manner.

[2]Meaning locality or village levels.

[3]By the time the allocations studied in this book have been made.

One additional information, which has already been mentioned. This book has been entirely self-funded. This has produced clear limitations in exploring additional timely opportunities for data collection, especially in order to complement in a qualitative approach the extensive quantitative databases that have been analysed. Yet, this has also meant that the author had more degrees of freedom for the general approach of the study, as well as for testing various prediction models.

Chapter 3
Study Context

3.1 Overview of Romanian Local Public Administration

The Romanian public administration system consists of a two-tier local government structure including 3181 municipalities (3180 municipalities plus the municipality of Bucharest, the capital city) and 41 county councils. The set of 3181 municipalities includes 2861 rural municipalities, 217 towns and 103 cities.[1] Both the local and county councils are elected. The local council consists of 9–31 members, while the county council consists of 31–37 members. Both local and county councils usually meet once a month in ordinary meetings, if necessary. The members of the local council are elected by secret ballot and by direct suffrage.

While there are no subordination relationships between the county and the local councils, the legal provisions in the Romanian Constitution state that the county council is the public administration authority to coordinate the activities of the municipalities (commune, town and municipal councils) in order to provide services at county level (Article 122).

The executive bodies of the local and county councils are represented by the mayor, respectively, the President of the County Council.

In terms of size, there is a large number of municipalities under or equal to 5000 inhabitants (Table 3.1).[2] Together they account for more than one-third of the population of the total number of 3180 municipalities (excluding the capital city, the municipality of Bucharest). These include a total number of 29 urban municipalities (out of the total number of 2491 municipalities under or equal to 5000 inhabitants). The importance of the size of local governments has been related to the relation between the optimal size of sub-central governments and the assignment of public expenditures so that 'that provision is the responsibility of the jurisdiction

[1] Annex to Law no. 290/2018, Statistical situation documentary on administrative organisation of Romania's territory.

[2] Public sector employment by central and local public administration is provided in Table 3.2.

A. M. Marin, *Assessing PNDL*, https://doi.org/10.1007/978-3-030-82844-8_3

Table 3.1 Breakdown of municipalities according to the size of the population

Number of inhabitants	Number of municipalities	Out of which, urban municipalities	Percentage of total population
Under 2000	752	1	6.08
2001–5000	1739	28	30.57
5001–10,000	479	105	17.33
10,001–20,000	115	91	8.18
20,001–100,000	076	75	17.19
Over 100,001	19	19	20.65
Total	3180	319	100

Source: Author's calculations based on data from the Population Census of 2011. Note: the municipality of Bucharest is not included in the analysis (municipality over 100,001 inhabitants)

Table 3.2 Public sector employment by central and local public administration

Level of public administration	No. of people employed	% of public sector employment
Local	672,062	56.67%
Central	513,938	43.33%
Total	1,186,000	100%

Source: Council of Europe (2014), 44

representing the smallest possible area over which the benefits are distributed' (Oates apud Darby et al. 2003; Swianiewicz et al. 2017).

According to the Framework Law on decentralisation (No. s195/2006), there is no hierarchical relationship between local authorities and county council or between the local council and mayor. Towns, cities, municipalities and counties can decide on matters of general interest, in areas under their jurisdiction, in accordance with the law.

Previous studies on local development in Romania highlight the need to coordinate funding opportunities for local communities. This is the case of the World Bank studies on Coordination of Strategies and Programs (2015) as well as the background study conducted for developing Improved Prioritisation Criteria for PNDL projects (2014). Based on the findings provided by the WB studies, the latest assessment on the state of the territory stresses that: 'As regards funding for roads rehabilitation, there are relatively few cases in which a road rehabilitated/ upgraded with European funds (2007–2013) to be complemented by another road linkage rehabilitated/ modernized by PNDL funds' (Ministry of Regional Development and Public Administration, 2018, 66). In addition, the background studies (Popescu-Criveanu et al., 2014, 6) for substantiating the Strategy for territorial development in Romania emphasise that there are significant disparities in what concerns the size and distribution of localities in the territory, as follows:

- There is a significant number of towns declining in terms of population—119 towns with a population under 10,000 inhabitants (minimum threshold set in the Law no. 315/2001)

- There are 6 urban localities under 3000 inhabitants and 15 towns between 3000 and 5000 inhabitants. The smallest towns by population size are Băile Tuşnad (Harghita county), Vaşcău and Nucet (Bihor county).
- There are rural municipalities nearby urban localities which are in rapid development, with a structure of facilities and services not matching the expanding size of the population.
- There is a set of new towns developed close to large municipalities such as Bucharest, Piteşti and Braşov.
- The way the resources are distributed in the territory and population movement resulted in the design of large multifunctional localities and small mono-functional localities, that concluded in a disproportionate distribution of resources in the territory as well as significant discrepancies in regard to housing quality and opportunities offered by the two categories of urban localities.

Within the European context, Romania ranks a medium degree of local autonomy, with values between 50 and 60, alongside Slovak Republic, Portugal, Belgium, Netherlands, Macedonia, Croatia, Luxembourg, Latvia and Spain (Ladner et al., 2015, 64). The countries with the highest autonomy levels (values above 70) are the Nordic countries—Denmark, Finland, Sweden, Norway and Iceland, and also Switzerland, Germany, as well as a former post-communist country like Poland. Furthermore, another post-communist country like Hungary ranks among countries with medium-low degree of autonomy (values between 40 and 50). The local autonomy is a composite index based on seven dimensions:

- legal autonomy refers to the position given to the municipalities within the state;
- organisational autonomy measures the extent to which local authorities are able to decide aspects of their political system and their own administration;
- policy scope includes the range of functions or tasks where municipalities are effectively involved in the delivery of services;
- effective political discretion analyses the range of tasks over which local government effectively has a say and whether it enjoys a general competence clause;
- financial autonomy (related to fiscal autonomy, financial self-reliance and borrowing autonomy) combines variables related to financial resources of local government giving them the possibility to influence their own budget;
- central or regional control (financial transfer systems and administrative supervision) combines the importance given to the municipalities within the state and the extent to which municipalities are controlled by higher levels of the state;
- vertical influence (central or regional access) measures the extent to which municipalities are able to influence political decisions on higher levels (ibid.).

Out of these dimensions, this study considers mostly aspects related to fiscal autonomy—within the set of tested independent variables, central control and vertical influence—in the description of the institutional environment/ organisational field for PNDL funding.

The dimensions of the institutional setting in which mayors act in European countries are taken into consideration in the development of the typologies of local government systems. Both horizontal and vertical power relations are examined. Horizontal power relations relate to the relationships between the mayor, the council and the municipal administration, and the vertical power relations to the relation and competencies/autonomy and control of the local level within the political system of the country (Heinelt et al., 2018, 20). The study mentioned above makes a typology of local government systems based on three dimensions: (1) institutional dimension, with distinctions between unitary-centralised, unitary-decentralised and federal systems of public administration; (2) cultural dimension—distinctions made between Continental European culture or 'rule of law' and Anglo-Saxon public interest culture, managerialism; (3) historical dimension differentiating between classic (Western) bureaucratic models and post-communism, including administrative transformation/system change as well as different pre-communist administrative traditions (Heinelt et al., 2018: 50–51). Based on these dimensions, Romania is considered as part of the cluster of South-East European (SEE) type—Bulgaria, Croatia, Romania and Slovenia.

In the strategic context framework, the present Strategy for strengthening public administration (2014–2020) states among its objectives increased efficiency of allocation and spending of public funds. It also provides a vision in which, by 2020, public administration in Romania will undergo a spiral of trust in regard to the society, in which the beneficiaries will enjoy integrated public services, appropriate and of high quality, delivered, after a rigorous testing of options, by public pro-active authorities and institutions that are supportive to change (p.6).

Additionally, the general context in which local governments act at a national level is also dependent on other factors, such as:

- Direct or indirect method of electing municipal leaders. Direct election is the case of Eastern Europe countries such as Hungary, Poland, Romania, Slovakia and Slovenia, and a few Western ones[3] (European Commission, 2016, 189). In relation to PNDL, this difference is closely related to, on the one hand, the strategic choices the mayors act upon in their endeavour to be re-elected. On the other hand, the method for electing the president of the second tier of the local government is also important. In Romania, the president and the vice presidents of the County Council are elected, by secret ballot, with the majority of votes of the county councillors elected by the population (by list of Parties). The present study considers variables related to political affiliation of the president of the County Council, as well as to his experience (length of tenure as President of the County Council).
- The share of public investment managed by local governments in each country. The same EU study shows, for Romania's case, a significant increase in the public investment from 2005 to 2015, yet below the increase registered, for instance,

[3] Italy, most of the German and Austrian Länder, as well as a few UK districts.

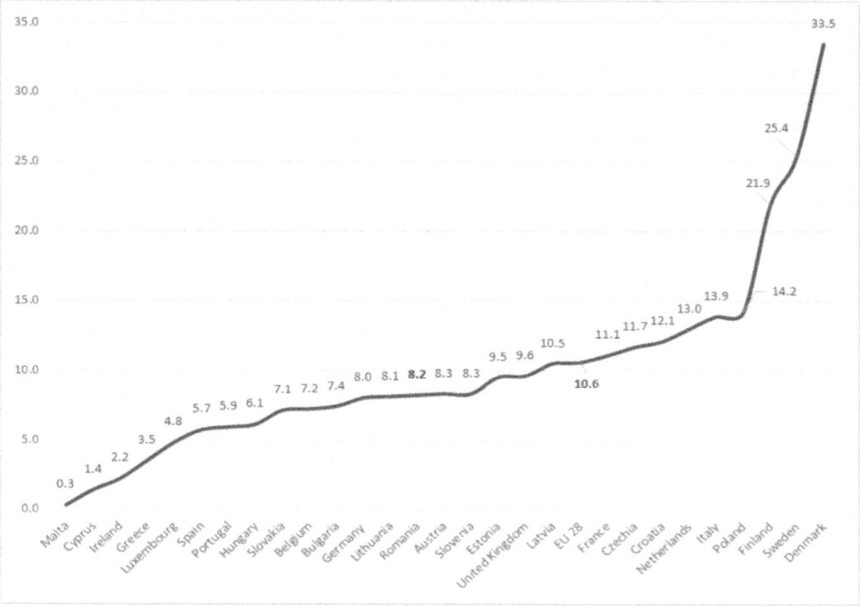

Fig. 3.1 Local Government Expenditure in EU—2018 (% of GDP). Source: Eurostat (gov_10a_main). Date of access: August 16, 2019

in Bulgaria. In Bulgaria and Romania, for example, the share increased by 2.4 and 3.3% points, respectively, between 2005 and 2015, with this increase partly explained by the funds absorbed and spent from Cohesion Policy (European Commission, 2016, 192). Nevertheless, both countries started from a very low level in 1995. In Romania's case, one special mention has to be paid for the year of 1999, which marks the start of fiscal decentralisation in Romania. The Law no. 189/1998 on local public finances was firstly applied in 1999. Starting with that year, new responsibilities have been transferred to the local government, but also a new revenue structure for the local governments has been introduced.

- Local authority expenditure as a share of both national GDP and total public spending as indicators of their role in policy implementation. Concerning the level of local government expenditure, Romania ranks on a rather average level as a share of GDP (with 8.2% in 2018 as compared to 10.6% in the EU—Fig. 3.1). Yet, this share is low compared to other post-communist countries like Poland (14.2%) and the Czech Republic (11.7%). The value for Romania is rather similar to Slovenia (8.3) and higher than that for Bulgaria (7.4%) and Hungary (6.1%). In addition, the value for Romania is in a slow decrease in the period of 2009–2018 (from 9.5 in 2009 and 10.4 in 2011), while in Hungary the decrease is very sharp—from 11.9% in 2009 and 12.5 in 2010. In this respect, in the EC study (2016) Romania is included in type 4, with a low share of GDP (less than 10%) and a medium share of public spending (over 20%). This type also includes

Estonia, Latvia, Lithuania and Switzerland. Such a combination of the levels for these two indicators outlines that local public authorities represent minor players in policy implementation and the delivery of services.
- The share of locally controlled revenues in the total local revenues as an indicator of their financial autonomy. For the year of 2014, Romania is included among the group of countries with low financial autonomy, where local authorities derive fewer than 25% of their total revenues (European Commission, 2016, 195). This group also includes Bulgaria, Estonia, Lithuania, Malta and the Netherlands. Other post-communist countries like Hungary and Poland are among countries with moderate financial autonomy, while the Czech Republic, Slovenia and Latvia are included in the group of high financial autonomy. This study takes into consideration variables related to local financial autonomy, measured as the share of local revenues in the total budget or as the level of total revenues per capita.
- Spending freedom as another indicator of municipal financial autonomy, depends on two elements: (a) the percentage of locally controlled revenues (taxes and fees) out of the total revenue; and (b) the degree of flexibility in using transfers from higher levels of government. Figure 3.2 presents the distribution of local revenues[4] in the total budget at the level of all county councils in Romania. Data are for 2017 and illustrate county councils' fiscal autonomy taken into consideration in PNDL II allocations studied by this book.

Likewise, the indicators mentioned above, Romania also ranks low on this indicator—meaning low share of locally controlled revenues and low flexibility in the use of financial transfers from higher levels of government. This group also includes Austria, Germany, Hungary, the Netherlands and the UK.

As a conclusion, Romanian local authorities rank low concerning their financial autonomy and spending freedom, which significantly limits their fiscal space and choices for funding needed objective investments in their communities.

3.2 Context of the State Budget Funded Programs

PNDL is the main funding source for local infrastructure. Its basic principle is that each locality in the country should have ensured a set of minimum public services (10s), in the following fields: health, education, water and sewerage, thermal and electric heating, including public lighting, transport/ roads, sanitation, culture, religion, housing and sport. The second stage of program implementation funds 9500 investment objectives, out of which 2500 nursery and kindergartens, 2000 schools and 5000 other objectives (of all eligible fields). For all these investments,

[4]For further details, see the definition of fiscal capacity in Romania.

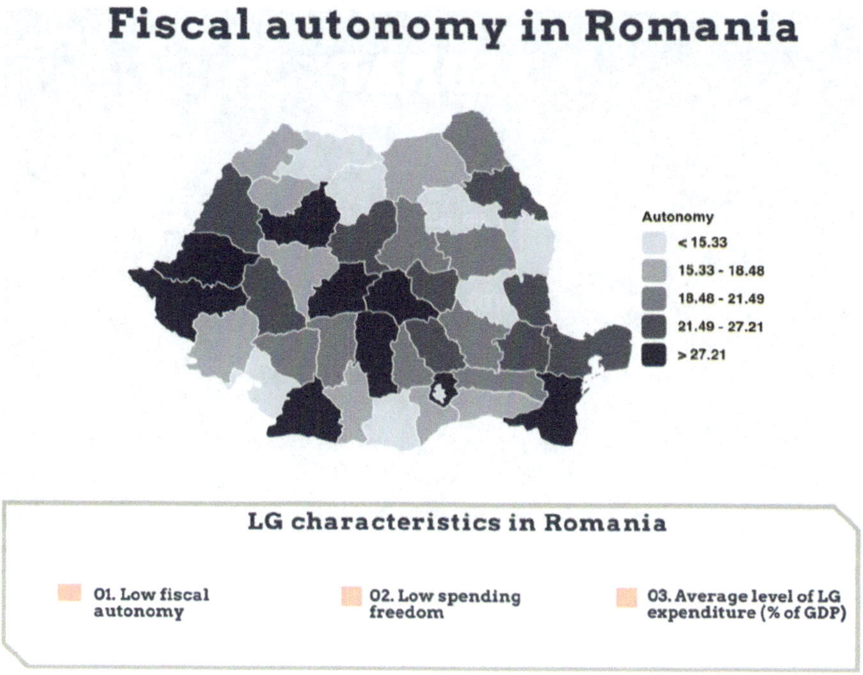

Fig. 3.2 Fiscal autonomy of County Councils in Romania. Source: Map elaborated by the author, based on local budgets execution data. Note: The map presents the share of local revenues in the total budget for all County Councils in Romania, for the year of 2017, prior to PNDL II allocations

there is a total budget fund allocated of approximately 30 billion lei commitment appropriations.[5]

Alongside PNDL, there are other funding lines from State Budget, like those managed by the National Company for Investments—CNI. CNI manages the National Program for Investments in Buildings of Public or Social Interest (PNCIPS) which implements investment objectives according to Annex 3 from GO 25/2001, with subsequent modifications. The Program funds various types of investments: (1) building new objectives; (2) rehabilitation, upgrading and endowment for investments; (3) rehabilitation, upgrading, endowment and extending the investment; (4) finalisation and (5) equipment.[6] The list of projects from CNI[7] includes a list of 6831 investments; yet, these are in different stages of

[5]Source: PNDL presentation available on the website of Ministry of Regional Development and Public Administration, available at: http://www.mdrap.ro/lucrari-publice/pndl (date of access: June 8, 2018).

[6]Source: https://www.cni.ro/proiecte/proiecte.

[7]Date of access: June 3, 2020.

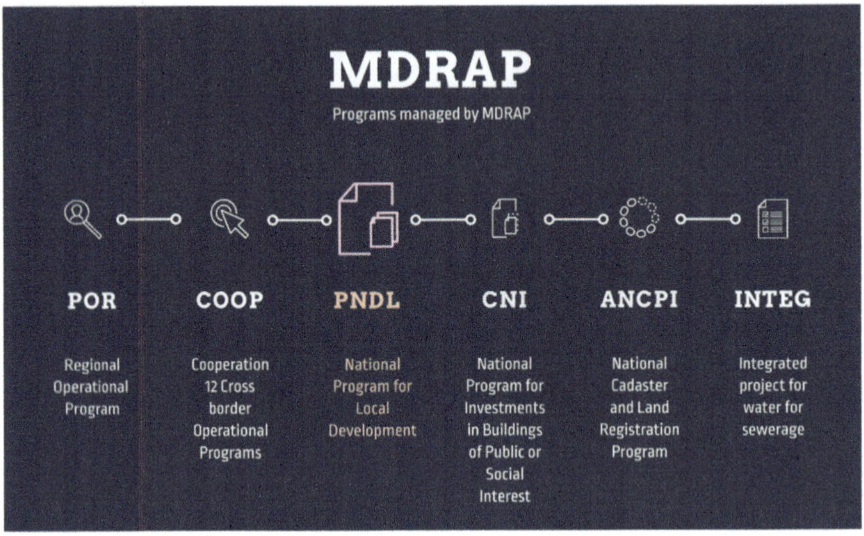

Fig. 3.3 Programs managed by MDRAP. Source: Author based on the information provided on the Ministry website: https://www.mlpda.ro/ (date of access: September 23, 2020)

finalisation. Some of them have no clear total sum of investments attached for each investment objective. To add even more elusiveness, there is no clear beneficiary of the investment (county council, administrative-territorial unit, NGO, county school inspectorate, etc.), and a significant part of the objectives have no explicit status—to give but few examples—submitted, approved, finalised, etc. The types of investment objectives include water and sewerage systems, sports facilities, cultural objectives (including churches), local roads, but also hospitals, educational institutions, etc. In order to get a clearer picture, CNI is a public institution under the authority of the Ministry of Regional Development and Public Administration.

Extensive State Budget and European funds are managed by the same Ministry, the Ministry of Regional Development and Public Administration (MDRAP), as shown in Fig. 3.3. Large infrastructure European-funded programs like the Regional Operational Program (POR) 2014–2020 is managed by the same Ministry. The Regional Operational Program funds similar investment objectives to PNDL, namely county roads by Priority Axis 6 and educational infrastructure by Priority Axis 10. In addition, Cross Border Co-Operation programs also fund road infrastructure from bordering counties. These are twelve operational programs and are managed by the same Ministry, MDRAP. In addition, the Operational Program for Large Infrastructure (POIM) finances investments in water and sewerage infrastructure, yet it is managed by a different Ministry. Furthermore, the National Rural Development Program also funds investments in the rural areas, including roads, water and sewerage or educational units.

In order to further illustrate the degree in which the control of a resource is concentrated, Fig. 3.3 also includes programs managed by organisations under subordination/coordination of the same Ministry. These are represented by the National Company for Investments (CNI) and the National Agency for Cadastre and Land Register (ANCPI). The latter institution manages a national-level program which is highly important for eligibility requirements in accessing funds by the local authorities. Bottlenecks related to land registration have been previously identified in relation to European-funded projects (Marin, 2016). Further on, a Department[8] from the same Ministry, together with CNI, manages an integrated project for water and sewage, thus covering investment objectives similar to those funded by PNDL, the Operational Program for Large Infrastructure (POIM), the National Company for Investments (CNI) or the National Plan for Rural Development (PNDR). This program is funded through a combination of funds from the Development Bank of the Council of Europe, State Budget and local authorities. It funds 74 localities from 20 counties, with a population of under 50,000 inhabitants.[9]

The following example (Box 3.1) illustrates the case of a complex investment objective which has been eligible for various funding lines, yet succeeded in securing funding only after a long term. The key problem is not that there are various funding lines available for local authorities.[10] As explained in the section on *Why study State Budget funded programs and PNDL?*, there still is a significant funding gap for covering the needs of local infrastructure in Romania. The main issue is the lack of coordination among them which, in the case of PNDL, is further worsened by a lack of transparency of published information and clear selection criteria.

Box 3.1 One Investment Objective, Multiple Funding Lines

The Technical Economic Commission from the Ministry of Public Works, Development and Administration (MLPDA)[a] approved the technical and economic indicators of the public investment on rehabilitation and consolidation of the National College Carol I and Romanian Opera House from Craiova municipality, Dolj county. The objective is included in the National Program for Investments in Buildings of Public or Social Interest, implemented by the National Company for Investments (CNI).

The estimated total value is 115,528,699 lei, and the total timeframe for implementation is 30 months, out of which six are for design activities.

In the near future, according to the legal provisions, the investment objective is about to be submitted for approval by the Inter-Ministerial

(continued)

[8]General Department of Regional Development and Infrastructure.

[9]Source: Ministry of Public Works, Development and Administration—MLDPA (former MDRAP): https://www.mlpda.ro/uploads/articole/attachments/5dc41bbae1b6a896485404.pdf (date of access: September 24, 2020).

[10]Another example with multiple funding lines is provided in Fig. 3.4.

Fig. 3.4 Projects on sewerage network and wastewater treatment from the municipality of Alba Iulia. Source: World Bank (2015, 33)

Box 3.1 (continued)

Committee for Approving Public Works of National Interests and Housing, after which, technical and economic indicators will be approved by issuing a Governmental Decision, which will further on result in starting a public procurement procedure initiated by CNI, on contracting design and implementation works.

Source: https://www.cni.ro/noutati/comunicate-de-presa/-id-65-cmsid-66 (date of access: June 3, 2020)

(continued)

Box 3.1 (continued)

This deplorable status of the building nowadays could have been avoided if European funds from the Regional Operational Program 2007–2013 would have been absorbed, through which also the Art Museum from Craiova has been rehabilitated. That was the only opportunity to rehabilitate it. Since then, other European funds for monuments have been available, but without being for educational units and they were all up to five million euro including the co-funding sum, much less than the sum necessary for rehabilitating the College and the Opera—which is of about approximately 24 million euro.

There was another axis through European funds for educational units, but this axis is for technical colleges, and Carol I College is not eligible here, it is a theoretical one. Furthermore, it is one funding objective which cannot be compared with other types of projects because it has an increased functional complexity—it included two institutions with two different functionalities—an educational and a cultural unit, but also as a result of the huge amount needed for its rehabilitation.

Previous endeavours (selection):

2017: there are two public procurement procedures with funds from the local budget initiated at the level of Craiova Mayoralty (minimum level option). Based on the information from SEAP[b] with nr. 176441 from June 23, 2017 and nr. 179058 from September 21, 2017, none of the participants in the procedure complied with the requirements set by the local public authority.

2018: Craiova Mayoralty asks the National Company of Investments, through an official letter no. 32258/February 21, 2018, to include the rehabilitation of Carol I College and Romanian Opera House from Craiova within the National Program for Public or Social Interest Constructions.

Source: www.primariacraiova.ro/ro/comunicate-de-presa/demersuri-efectuate-pentru-reabilitarea-cladirii-colegiului-naional-carol-i.html (date of access: June 3, 2020)

N.G.: As a result of a characteristic vigilance, all MPs from PSD[c] Dolj left the room before I would support this amendment. Don't you think this is just a coincidence? But ....

N.G. This is the kind of consideration they have for the ones who elected them.

N.G. Amendment no. 1.163.

N.G. National College Carol I from Craiova is the most prestigious school in Oltenia and one of the most important in Romania. The building is from 1842 and has been painted by Theodor Aman in his famous painting 'Hora Unirii in Craiova'. It is considered a historical monument. Consequently, we suggest allocating 9.000 thousand lei for starting the rehabilitation works for Carol I College from the municipality of Craiova, Dolj county.

N.G. You should congratulate your colleagues from Dolj for the courage they had when faced with this amendment. (Applause. Clamours)

(continued)

Box 3.1 (continued)
Source: Parliamentary Debates. Common Meeting of Chamber of Deputies and Senate from February 14, 2019, http://www.cdep.ro/pls/steno/steno.stenograma?ids=8022&idl=1 (date of access: June 3, 2020)

[a]Former Ministry of Regional Development and Public Administration.

[b]Electronic System of Public Procurement.

[c]PSD—ruling party by the time this amendment was supported.

To sum up, this complex environment of funds means simultaneous availability of financial resources for the same potential beneficiaries (county councils, urban and rural municipalities) in a partial overlap between funding objectives (especially for road and water and sewerage infrastructure) as well as funding agencies. Amongst these, MDRAP represents an institution which concentrates a high degree of control over financial resources available for local public authorities at all levels in Romania.

3.3 Additional Method of Project Submission: The Role of MPs in Funding Local Public Authorities

PNDL is funded through State Budget transfers, within the limit annually approved in MLDPA (former MDRAP) budget, from funds annually approved with this destination in the local budgets of administrative-territorial units and other funding sources legally established, according to the Ministry's presentation of the program.[11] Within the limit of funds annually approved by State Budget Law, based on an internal analysis of the funding proposals received from local public authorities, MLDPA approves by Ministerial Order the final list with investment objectives funded by State Budget, to be published on Ministry website (ibid.). In short, the State Budget Law decides the total amount of funds available for PNDL. Nevertheless, as outlined in the report published by the Romanian Court of Accounts (2015), there has also been a significant time lag between the financial allocations (as stated in the Ministerial Order) and signing of the funding contracts, as well as no prioritisation criteria whenever supplementing or redistributing the funds.[12]

Additionally, as introduced in the previous section, the most surprising of all funding opportunities for local public authorities is not a specific (operational) program, but the intervention of the members of the Parliament as amendments submitted to the legislative framework (see also Box 3.1, in the previous section).

[11]Source: https://www.mlpda.ro/pages/programulnationaldezvoltarelocala (date of access: June 9, 2020).

[12]Analysis conducted for previous PNDL sessions, not for allocations conducted in PNDL II.

Interventions of the MPs in relation to PNDL regard the funds allocated through the State Budget Law. In order to illustrate this topic for the case of PNDL II, I have conducted a short analysis of verbatim transcripts of meetings in the Romanian Parliament, represented by the Senate and the Chamber of Deputies. The selection is based on texts searched by keywords like PNDL and PNDL II, for the transcripts publicly available. If one would extend the searched key words, it would most likely result in other funding opportunities available for mayors and the local communities they represent.

Previous studies (Marin, 2015) offered insights into the role of MPs in providing support for the absorption of European funds. Again, funding the needs of local communities is, of course, a positive thing. Yet, the process and the mechanism of funding these needs with the support of MPs reveal systemic challenges for local and central public administration in Romania. MPs interventions do not only increase the total amount proposed by the Government, but they also specify a list of 'winners' (see Box 3.2). Thus, their interventions bypass any formal funding programs and might introduce distortions in the overall fiscal policy concerning local public authorities. Namely, this brief analysis reveals the following:

- There are no clear projects guidelines when proposing these amendments. From this perspective, it seems like the simplest way to approving a 'project'. It looks like MPs already have a clear diagnosis of the situation as well as of the appropriate measures to undertake in each community.
- Identified amendments do not refer to a competition between various local public authorities, but for 'already decided winners'—specific funding lines. It can be noticed from the following excerpts that there really is a strong connection between certain MPs and the funding opportunities at the local level for specific localities. Amendment approval in the Parliament of Romania depends on the overall political configuration and MP's political affiliation compared to the ruling party. This area requires further systematic investigation to check which share of the proposed amendments are actually adopted and implemented and from which MPs, counties, political parties and for which local communities.[13] A preliminary analysis shows that most proposed amendments are not approved.
- The selected amendments mainly refer to increasing MDRAP's budget (as a consequence of the selected keywords), but further investigation might yield insights about other State Budget funded programs. Thus, they refer to PNDL I, PNDL II and CNI's previously mentioned program on National Program for Investments in Buildings of Public or Social Interest (PNCIPS) or to simple specific needs of particular localities. One MP even says that he suggests some projects which have not been funded from PNDL II in the first session ('as a result of lack of funding') to be included in the next session. Again, this approach would entirely exclude a complex schema of prioritisation criteria.

[13] From the ones listed in Box 3.2, it looks like only a few have been accepted.

Box 3.2 MP's Role in PNDL II and Other Funding Sources for Local Public Authorities

.S. At the position 706 ... it is at the Ministry of Development, but from CNI budget, funding for the investment objective 'Sports facility of touristic interest in the commune of Rodna, Bistriţa-Năsăud county', with the sum of 5360 thousand lei. Please approve this amendment because this commune has been developed based on mining. All the mines from that area have been closed. It is the only chance that this commune would develop in the future, and please give a positive vote.[d]

D.B. Thank you, Mr. President. I will not suggest a set of 10 amendments for funding the investment objectives requested by the administrative units from Argeş. For the first eight of them, the corresponding mayoralties submitted, in the year of 2017, necessary documentation for obtaining the necessary funding from the Local Development National Fund—PNDL II. Unfortunately, their requests have been rejected due to lack of financial resources for the corresponding year. No. crt. 1.072

D.B. It is proposed to allocate the sum of 9088 thousand lei for funding the investment objective of 'Sewerage Network and sanitation station in the village of Boteşti, commune of Boteşti', Argeş county ....

D.B. No. crt. 1073. It is proposed to allocate the sum of 9600 thousand lei for funding the investment objective 'Sewerage and household wastewater treatment in the commune of Poienarii de Argeş, Argeş county'.

D.B. No. crt. 1074. It is proposed to supplement the funds provisioned in the Annex no. 3/15—Ministry of Regional Development and Public Administration—with the sum of 11,545 thousand lei for funding the investment objective 'Extending the sewerage network in the commune of Valea Iaşului', Argeş county.

D.B. No. crt. 1075. It is proposed to supplement the funds provisioned in the Annex no. 3/15—Ministry of Regional Development and Public Administration—with the sum of 7107 thousand lei for funding the investment objective 'Upgrading of communal roads DC 188 Ciomăgeşti-Dogari, the border with Olt county, the total length of 7.5 km, in the commune of Ciomăgeşti, Argeş county'.

D.B. No. crt. 1076. It is proposed to supplement the funds provisioned in the Annex no. 3/15—Ministry of Regional Development and Public Administration—with the sum of 9535 thousand lei for funding the investment objective 'Upgrading of communal roads in the commune of Izvoru, Argeş county'.

(continued)

Box 3.2 (continued)

D.B. No.crt.1077. It is proposed to allocate the sum of 584 thousand lei for funding the investment objective 'Upgrading of communal roads DC 101A in the commune of Mozăceni, Argeş county'.

D.B. No.crt. 1078. It is proposed to supplement the funds provisioned in the Annex no. 3/15—Ministry of Regional Development and Public Administration—with the sum of 7500 thousand lei for funding the investment objective 'Upgrading and rebuilding of DC 161 Cătunaşi, between the positions 3+100—3.270, in the area of landslides in the commune of Poiana Lacului, Argeş county'.

D.B. No.crt. 1079. It is proposed to supplement the funds provisioned in the Annex no. 3/15—Ministry of Regional Development and Public Administration—with the sum of 5443 thousand lei for funding the investment objective 'Upgrading of communal roads with a total length of 6 km, in the commune of Ştefan cel Mare, Argeş county'.

D.B. No.crt. 1080. It is proposed to supplement the funds provisioned in the Annex no. 3/15—Ministry of Regional Development and Public Administration—with the sum of 2161 thousand lei for funding the investment objective 'Upgrading of Communal Road 84 Ţiţeşti—School Valea Mânăstirii km. 3+250–km. 4+370, commune of Ţiţeşti, Argeş county'.

D.B. And the last amendment No.crt. 1.081. It is proposed to supplement the funds provisioned in the Ministry of Regional Development and Public Administration—with the sum of 2100 thousand lei for funding the investment objective 'Sport hall in the commune of Schitu Goleşti, Argeş county'. I would like to mention in the written material that, for all these amendments, there are motivations which are, from my point of view, extremely serious. In fact, you, as an Argeş senator, you know very well the situation. ...

L.D.L. It is proposed to supplement the sum provisioned in the Annex no.3/15 ...

L.D.L. 1102.

L.D.L. National Program of Local Development—with the sum of 300 thousand lei for modernisation (upgrading works)—road and bridge in the commune of Făurei, Neamţ county.

L.D.L. ... it passed.

L.D.L. 1.103. It is proposed to supplement the sum provisioned in the Annex no. 3/15, Chapter 5.001, National Program for Local Development, with the sum of 9498.470 thousand lei for setting up the water system and extending the sewerage in the wastewater treatment for the villages of Horia, Neamţ county.

L.D.L. 1.107. It is proposed to supplement the sum provisioned in the Annex no. 3/15, Chapter 5.001, National Program for Local Development,

(continued)

Box 3.2 (continued)
with the sum of 183 thousand lei for upgrading the communal road from Icuşeşti commune, Neamţ county…

C.I.I. 1.193. It is about another locality, which is in fact part of the municipality of Bistriţa, 10 km away. It is requested to allocate the sum of 50 thousand lei for funding the objective 'Sanitary installation…'. The funds are to be cut from the Ministry of Regional Development and Public Administration by transfers between public administration units—PNDL II.

N.N. The funds allocated through the National Program for Public Interest Constructions—National Company for Investments—4.650 thousand lei—construction of a swimming pool in the municipality of Mediaş, Sibiu county.

C.S. It is requested to supplement the sums necessary for constructing housing for youth with the purpose of renting them. Taking into consideration the high number of youths, we request for the municipality of Medias, through the Governmental program implemented by the National Agency for Housing, to supplement the sum with 19,600 thousand.

Source: Parliamentary Debates. Common Meeting of Chamber of Deputies and Senate from February 14, 2019 http://www.cdep.ro/pls/steno/steno2015.stenograma?ids=8022&idl=1 (date of access: June 3, 2020)

[d]This amendment has been approved.

This section is not intended to say that MPs have a decisive role in PNDL II allocations. It is just used as an example of how project proposals to be funded from PNDL II have an additional 'submission' procedure. As explained in the second section on Methodology, the quantitative analysis considered in this book solely uses PNDL II allocations as publicly displayed by the responsible Ministry, Ministry of Regional Development and Public Administration.

> 'MPs should not have any role in funds' allocation; they should be concerned with better regulation. If we look at the budgets from the last 25 years, thousands of amendments have been submitted, but what has been submitted has not been taken into consideration. If there is a parliamentary majority, one should support Government's project, what's the use of submitting amendments.' (Mayoralty representative, North-West development region)

3.4 PNDL Program Design: Steps for Allocating PNDL Funds

Despite improvements in allocation criteria following WB's recommendations, the transparency of program design documents is lagging behind. There is no clear and public strategic document nor an operational framework to accompany the implementation of this program.

The key legislative framework governing its implementation is represented by the Governmental Emergency Ordinance (GEO) no. 28/2013 on approving PNDL

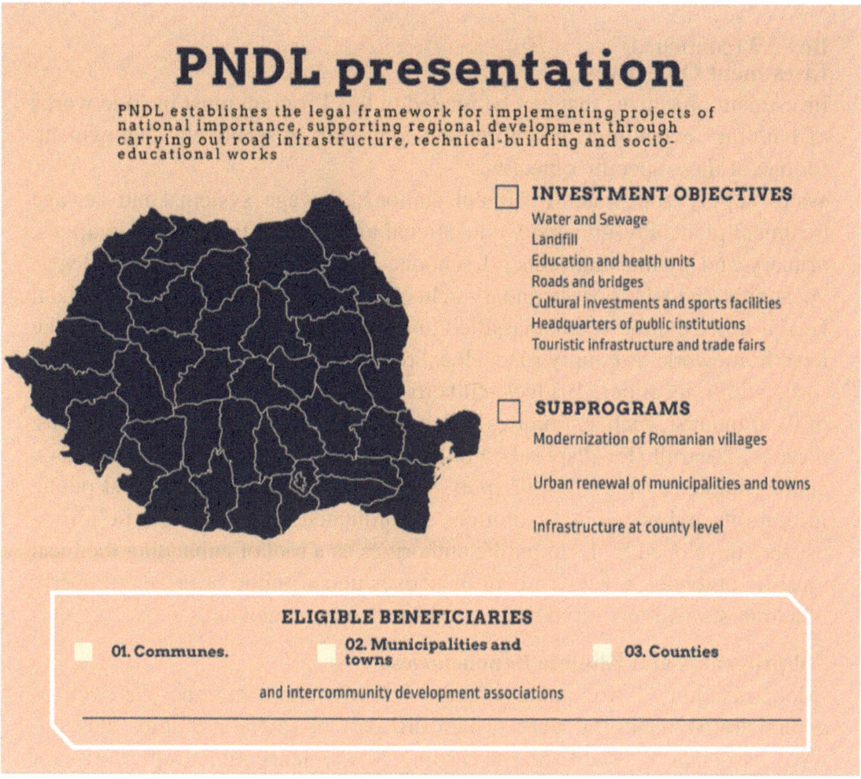

Fig. 3.5 PNDL presentation

and Order no. 1851/2013 on approving the methodological norms for implementing GEO no. 28/2013. The new version of selection criteria is included in the Governmental Decision no. 624/2015. The key features of the program are presented in Fig. 3.5, localities with allocations in Fig. 3.6, while further explanations are provided in Box 3.3 and subsequent text.

Box 3.3 PNDL General Presentation

Program Presentation
National Program for Local Development, coordinated by the Ministry of Public Works, Development and Administration,[e] establishes the legal framework for implementing projects of national importance, supporting regional development through carrying out road infrastructure, technical-building and socio-educational works.

(continued)

Box 3.3 (continued)

Investment Objectives

Investment objectives that can be funded in this Program must include works of building/ extending/ rehabilitation/ upgrading, respectively, endowment, for one of these specific objectives:

Water supply and water treatment stations; Sewage systems and sewage treatment plants Pre-university educational units, respectively: kindergartens, primary and gymnasium general schools, school groups, national colleges, vocational schools, postsecondary schools, special education State Budget; Health units; Public roads classified and registered, in accordance with the legal framework, as county roads, local roads, communal roads and/or public roads within localities; Bridges, culverts or overpasses; Cultural investments of local interest, such as libraries, museums, multifunctional cultural centres, theatres; Landfill (for disposal); Public and commercial markets, trade fairs, animal markets; Upgrading of sports facilities; Headquarters of local public institutions and of public institutions subordinated to them; Touristic infrastructure developed by local public authorities as a tool of enhancing the local touristic potential, for investment objectives under public or private property of administrative-territorial units or under their management.

Subprograms and Eligible Beneficiaries

'Modernisation of Romanian village' subprogram: communes, as well as administrative-territorial units which are part of intercommunity development association, established according to the legislative framework, for investments implemented by intercommunity development associations, represented by the local public authorities of communes;

'Urban renewal of municipalities and towns' subprogram: municipalities and towns, including component villages, as well as administrative-territorial units which are part of intercommunity development association, established according to the legislative framework, for investments implemented by intercommunity development associations, represented by local public authorities of municipalities, including their administrative-territorial subdivisions, of towns, including the villages which are part of them; 'Infrastructure at county level' subprogram: county local public authorities, as well as administrative-territorial units members of intercommunity development association, established according to the legislative framework, for investments implemented by intercommunity development associations, represented by county local public authorities. Source: https://www.mlpda.ro/pages/programulnationaldezvoltarelocala (date of access: June 9, 2020)

[c]Former Ministry of Regional Development and Public Administration (MDRAP).

Fig. 3.6 Distribution of investment objectives funded by PNDL II. Source: PNDL presentation. Map available at: https://www.gov.ro/fisiere/stiri_fisiere/15-04_Prezentare_MDRAP_ref_stadiul_PNDL.pdf (date of access: September 23, 2020). Note: the map marks territorial administrative units with funding from PNDL 2, not the volume of funds awarded for each locality

Here there is a need to make one special mention. A previous audit of PNDL conducted by the Romanian Court of Accounts (2015) concluded, among others, that the legislative framework governing the program does not contain enough elements that would be necessary for a national program. These refer to the lack of a law[14] for approving the program. This regulatory statute would be necessary based on Constitution's provisions. Additional references have been made to the inclusion of ambiguous statements, lack of clear definitions for investment objectives supported by the Program, lack of clear objectives and associated indicators, lack of a set maximum threshold for specific potential beneficiaries, etc. (Romanian Court of Accounts, 2015, 18–19). Part of them holds true for the period analysed by this study, too. To be more explicit, the same source cites the Law on public finances as providing definitions for considering a program. A program represents an action or a coherent set of actions which refer to the same main authorising officer, designed for achieving an objective or a set of clearly marked objectives and for which program indicators to assess the results achieved are set, according to the funding limits approved (Law no. 500/2002). The key terms in the definition are related to objectives, results indicators and funding limits approved. Only recently, some results indicators have been published by the responsible Ministry, yet funding limits remain unclear. To cite only recent developments, the Government

[14] Instead of a Governmental Ordinance or Governmental Decision.

has supplemented the program budget for the third time in 1 year for the projects submitted in both phases. From the last budgetary supplements, most parts of funds go to the beneficiaries of PNDL II projects (August 2020). The supplementary funds come from the Government's Reserve Fund.

According to the official response received from the Ministry of Regional Development and Public Administration (MDRAP), there are several prioritisation criteria used for PNDL.[15] These are also mentioned in the legislative framework (GD no. 624/2015) and are represented by:

1. The balanced distribution of funds to counties, considering fulfilment of at least one of the following indicators:

   - Demographic and territorial administrative data of the counties as compared to the national-level data. The law mentions the following three indicators:

     (i) the weight of the administrative-territorial unit number in the county as a share of the total administrative-territorial unit number at the national level;
     (ii) the weight of the county population as a share of the total population of the country;
     (iii) the weight of the country area as a percentage of the total area of the country.

   - Financial capacity of territorial administrative units. In this respect, the legislative framework specifies that it considers the units' capacity to participate with funds from the local budget for achieving investment objectives.
   - Share of the number of ongoing investment objectives in implementation in every county. Under this dimension, two indicators are considered:

     (i) the number of ongoing investment projects for each county as a share of total ongoing investments at a national level;
     (ii) the funding needs for completing the investment projects not yet completed as a share of the total funding needs for completing the investment projects started and not completed at national level.

2. Priority of achieving investments objectives from the priority fields of activity. For the case of PNDL 2017–2020, fields like tourism, local cultural objectives, sports facilities and landfill have not been considered priorities.[16] The eligible funding requests for PNDL 2017–2020 included the following domains: water, sewerage, education units, health units, roads, bridges, landfill, cultural objectives, marketplaces, sports facilities, public institutions offices, public lighting, touristic infrastructure and integrated fields. Table 3.3 presents the number of

[15]The texts of the two public information requests submitted to the Ministry alongside the response to the second public information request are presented in the Annex.

[16]This represents the response to the first public information request. According to the official response received from the Ministry of Regional Development and Public Administration (MDRAP) no. 119307/19.10.2018, following a public information request. The text of the response to the second public information request is presented in the Annex.

Table 3.3 Status of eligible funding requests by field of activity submitted in PNDL 2017–2020

Field of activity	Number of funding requests	Sum of funding requests (lei)
Water	652	3.031.250.623,44
Sewerage	1002	9.917.591.194,01
Educational units	3087	6.419.964.522,54
Health units	706	1.776.001.577,30
Roads	4031	34.211.217.288,18
Bridges	713	2.001.049.673,51
Landfill	40	114.526.417,62
Cultural objectives	330	921.447.428,68
Market places	110	368.424.843,96
Sports facilities	312	598.593.038,7
Public institutions offices	398	936.475.528,97
Public street lighting systems	1144	1.498.069.229,21
Touristic infrastructure	55	615.317.815,22
Integrated fields	517	5.015.384.536,11
Total	13,097	67.425.313.717,45

Source: official response received from the Ministry of Regional Development and Public Administration (MDRAP) no. 119307/19.10.2018, following a public information request. Note: In addition to these 13097 eligible funding requests, another 98 requests were considered non-eligible for funding from PNDL 2017–2020 (ibid.)

received funding requests together with the corresponding funds per each field of activity.
3. Priority of achieving the investments objectives with the most advanced physical stage of completion;
4. Date of signing the contract for delivering the services or construction works;
5. Served population.

The same official response states that for allocating the funds in PNDL 2017–2020, a weighted average has been composed, made up of the following indicators:

- 25%—share of the number of territorial administrative units at a national level;
- 30%—share of county population in the total country population;
- 10%—share of county area in the total country area;
- 35%—coefficient determined by the inverse of collected county personal income tax as compared to the total volume of taxes.

Step 1 Priority for projects focusing on nursery schools and kindergartens, as well as schools without sanitary or emergency situations authorisation ⇒ SUM 1

Step 2
1. The sum allocated in Step 1 is deducted from the total amount allocated for each county ⇒ SUM 2;
2. 35% of SUM 2 is allocated for county roads and bridges ⇒ SUM 3;

3. County roads were selected based on the scoring provided in the report elaborated by the WB,[17] not to overlap with the projects funded by POR 2014–2020 and also according to a balanced county development;
4. Priority requests made by county councils for county roads have also been taken into consideration, given the fact that the projects for funding from POR 2014–2020 have not been selected yet.

Step 3

1. 50% of SUM 3 is allocated for water and sewerage projects;
2. First, projects for water or integrated projects for water and sewerage are allocated, in ascending order of revenues for each territorial administrative unit; initially, one project for each territorial administrative unit is allocated;
3. Secondly, projects for sewerage are allocated, in the descending order of population for each unit; initially, one project for each territorial administrative unit is allocated;[18]
4. Sewerage projects have not been funded for those localities with projects for water with a higher value than the level established for the category of water and sewerage, based on the statistical analysis of distribution for each county;
5. Sewerage projects have not been funded for those localities with integrated projects for water and sewerage.
6. If the threshold of 50% of SUM3 has not been achieved, the rest of the sum has been allocated, without further restrictions, in the ascending order of revenues for each administrative-territorial unit, as follows:

   (i) For projects on water or for integrated projects on water and sewerage;
   (ii) Sewerage projects, establishing sewerage projects for territorial administrative units above 2000 inhabitants, or if there are good reasons,[19] for those units below 2000 inhabitants.

Step 4

1. Sums requested for rural dispensaries are allocated in the ascending order of revenues for each administrative-territorial unit. For the urban hospitals (from towns), only those projects with relevant background information supporting funding priority and 'special situations of public health policy at national level', based on the Ministry of Health's responses, following the requests submitted by MDRAP, are funded. The county hospitals have been funded, excepting outpatient care services and emergency units.
2. Sums requested for bridges, except for the county bridges, have been funded. This objective has no other funding line from the State Budget.

---

[17] Burduja et al. (2015).

[18] Only the territorial administrative units above 2000 inhabitants have been taken into consideration. The Ministry (MDRAP) also states that those requests in which the investment costs/inhabitant are greater than the EC recommendations have not been selected for funding.

[19] In Romanian, 'in cazuri justificate'.

3. Sums for communal/ urban roads are allocated, in the ascending order of revenues for each administrative-territorial unit, provided that:
   (i) The criterion on financial sustainability of the investment is fulfilled.
   (ii) The allocated sums do not exceed the level established for each county (adding together all the funding allocation from previous steps).

Step 5

(i) The sums not allocated in previous phases (steps 4.1, 4.2, 4.3) have been allocated in the next phase.

As can be seen from Figs. 3.7 and 3.8 (*Steps for allocating funds from PNDL 2017–2020*), there is a rather complicated process for funding allocation within PNDL II. In addition, multiple funding environments co-exist ambiguously. Coordination of EU funds is taken into consideration, but in a rather vague manner, as in Step 2, the Ministry states that 'priority requests made by county councils for county roads have also been taken into consideration, given the fact that the projects for funding from POR 2014–2020 have not been selected yet'. In addition, in Step 5, 'if the funding request could prevent a smooth implementation for the European-funded projects, the project has not been selected for funding'. Hence, there is no clear indication of a standardised operationalisation of the criterion for coordination with EU funding.[20]

Lack of transparent data, especially on application procedures and selection results, represents one other key issue in relation to PNDL program as a whole. In this respect, Romania's policy documents on Open Government Partnership (National Action Plan 2018–2020) assert a specific objective regarding PNDL: improving transparency in allocations and acquisitions from national investment funds. The lead implementing agency is the Ministry of Regional Development and Public Administration (MDRAP), with Expert Forum (EFOR) as other actor involved. The document resumes as follows the problem to be addressed: 'at present, there is limited data on how the funds are allocated, on public procurements and implementation of projects made through the National Program for Local Development (PNDL). In this context, the real impact and effectiveness of the program are difficult to quantify' (Government of Romania, 2018: 23). Correspondingly, the activities envisaged for addressing these shortcomings include:

- Identification of data sets that can be put together based on legal regulations and the information produced in the procedures for the awarding, contracting, implementation and evaluation of investments (responsible parties: MDRAP and EFOR, to be completed in 2018)
- Organise a public debate on data sets and related procedures, including necessary legislative changes (responsible parties: MDRAP and EFOR, to be completed in 2019)
- Define procedures and publish data sets (responsible institution: MDRAP, to be completed in July 2019)
- Updating the data sets (responsible institution: MDRAP, to be completed in 2020).

---

[20]Results of the distribution are presented in Fig. 3.6.

Step 1. Priority for projects focusing on nursery schools and kindergartens, as well as schools without sanitary or emergency situations authorization ⇒ SUM 1

Step 2.

1. The sum allocated in Step 1 is deducted from the total amount allocated for each county ⇒ SUM 2;
2. 35% of SUM 2 is allocated for county roads and bridges ⇒ SUM 3;
3. County roads were selected based on the scoring provided in the report elaborated by the WB,[28] not to overlap with the projects funded by POR 2014-2020 and also according to a balanced county development;
4. Priority requests made by county councils for county roads have also been taken into consideration, given the fact that the projects for funding from POR 2014-2020 have not been selected yet.

Step 3.

1. 50% of SUM 3 is allocated for water and sewerage projects;
2. First, projects for water or integrated projects for water and sewerage are allocated, in ascending order of revenues for each territorial administrative unit; initially, one project for each territorial administrative unit is allocated;
3. Secondly, projects for sewerage are allocated, in the descending order of population for each unit; initially, one project for each territorial administrative unit is allocated;[29]
4. Sewerage projects have not been funded for those localities with projects for water with a higher value than the level established for the category of water and sewerage, based on the statistical analysis of distribution for each county;
5. Sewerage projects have not been funded for those localities with integrated projects for water and sewerage.
6. If the threshold of 50% of SUM3 has not been achieved, the rest of the sum has been allocated, without further restrictions, in the ascending order of revenues for each administrative territorial unit, as follows:

   (i) For projects on water or for integrated projects on water and sewerage;
   (ii) Sewerage projects, establishing sewerage projects for territorial administrative units above 2,000 inhabitants, or if there are good reasons,[30] for those units below 2,000 inhabitants.

Fig. 3.7 Steps for allocating funds in PNDL II (2017–2020) (According to the official response received from the Ministry of Regional Development and Public Administration (MDRAP) no. 119307/19.10.2018, following a public information request.)

Step 4.

1. Sums requested for rural dispensaries are allocated in the ascending order of revenues for each administrative territorial unit. For the urban hospitals (from towns), only those projects with relevant background information supporting funding priority and "special situations of public health policy at national level", based on the Ministry of Health's responses, following the requests submitted by MDRAP, are funded. The county hospitals have been funded, excepting outpatient care services and emergency units.
2. Sums requested for bridges, except for the county bridges, have been funded. This objective has no other funding line from the State Budget.
3. Sums for communal/ urban roads are allocated, in the ascending order of revenues for each administrative territorial unit, provided that:

   (i) The criterion on financial sustainability of the investment is fulfilled.
   (ii) The allocated sums do not exceed the level established for each county (adding together all the funding allocation from previous steps).

Step 5.

(i) The sums not allocated in previous phases (steps 4.1, 4.2, 4.3) have been allocated in the next phase.

Fig. 3.7 (continued)

The latest updates (November 2019) of information on both MDRAP and open governmental websites show no improvements concerning the envisaged advancements in the published information. This means that the structure of the published open data remains the same—the file on Investment Objectives funded by PNDL II (stage as of November 2019) includes the same variables as in the initial one published at the beginning of PNDL II, on which the analysis presented in this book relies.

In relation to data transparency, there is a good example worth mentioning, identified in the case of the report activity made public by the Prefecture from Satu Mare.[21] This is the type of report that puts together all the project proposals initiated, submitted, implemented, irrespective of their source of funding, as well as on the type of project phase. From this activity report, the following table presents only excerpts related to various projects submitted on PNDL by local councils or county council from Satu Mare county (Table 3.4). As can be noted from the below table, several projects have been submitted by county, or local councils, and only part of them have succeeded in securing funding from PNDL II. Investment objectives of

[21]Prefect's Institution (2017) available at: https://sm.prefectura.mai.gov.ro/wp-content/uploads/sites/32/2017/12/Realizari-9-luni-ultim-doc.compressed.pdf (date of access: June 16, 2020).

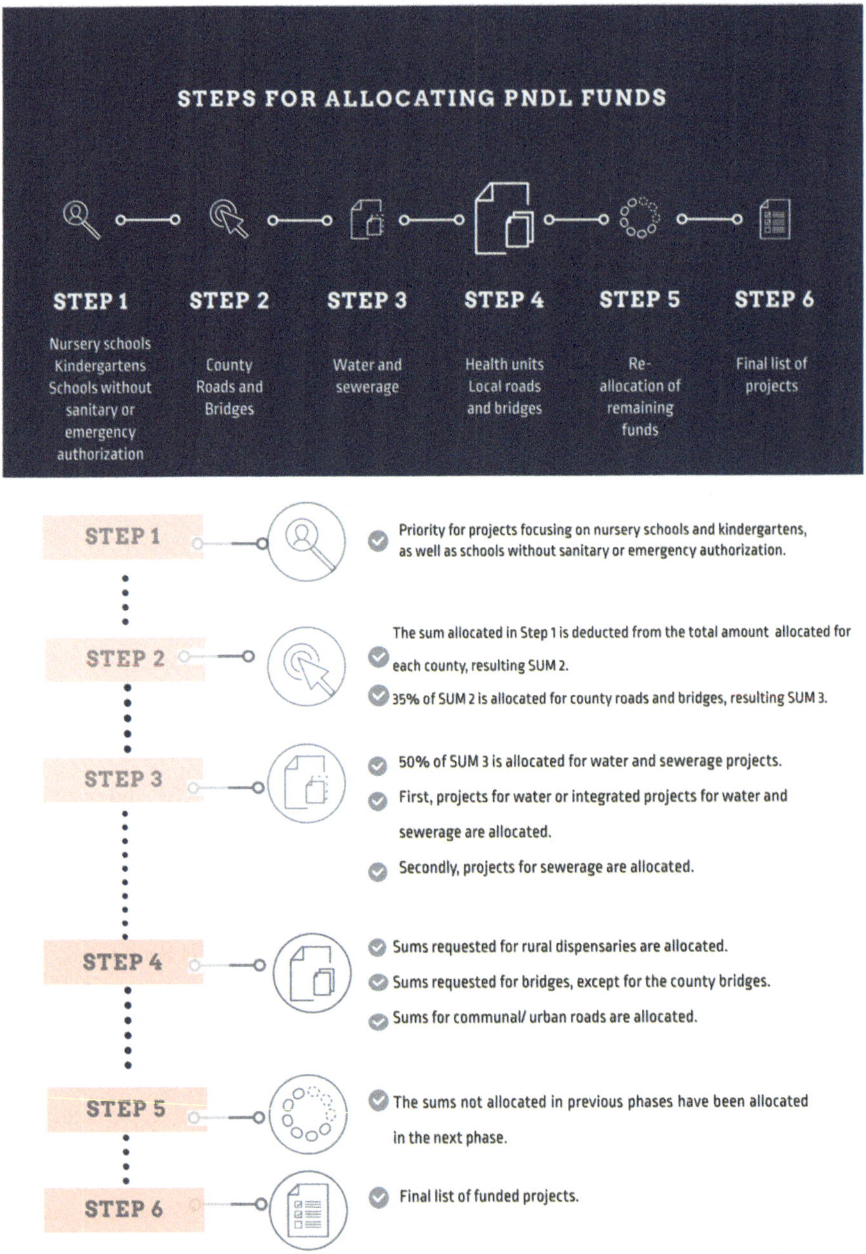

Fig. 3.8 Steps for allocating PNDL II funds. Source: Author based on the information provided in the answers to the public information requests submitted by MDRAP

Table 3.4 Excerpts from the list of projects submitted for funding from PNDL II in Satu Mare county

Project title	Applicant	Achievements after nine months
Enhancing the value of the historical monument Vecsey House—Satu Mare County Museum	Satu Mare County Council	Project submitted at MDRAPFE to be funded from PNDL II. The funding was not secured
Energy efficiency for County Emergency Hospital no. 1 Satu Mare, located on Ravesburg street no.2	Satu Mare County Council	The technical—economic documentation has been funded. It has been submitted at MDRAPFE to be funded by PNDL II. The funding was not secured from PNDL
Energy efficiency for County Emergency Hospital no. 2 Satu Mare located in Piaţa Eroilor Revoluţiei no.2–3	Satu Mare County Council	This objective has been considered by CNI.[a] It has been submitted at MDRAPFE to be funded by PNDL II. The funding was not secured from PNDL
Rehabilitation of the administrative office, P-ţa 25 octombrie, no. 1, Satu Mare	Satu Mare County Council	Submitted at MDRAPFE to be funded by PNDL II.
Upgrading of the mayoralty office for Pişcolt commune, Satu Mare county	Pişcolt Local Council	Funding request submitted at MDRAPFE to be included in PNDL II. No funding secured
Rehabilitation, upgrading and extension of the mayoralty of Terebeşti commune	Terebeşti Local Council	Funding request submitted at MDRAPFE to be included in PNDL II
Rehabilitation and equipment, extending the building of Tiream commune mayoralty, Satu Mare county	Tiream Local Council	A funding request to PNDL II was submitted in 2017. The project has not been approved
Thermal rehabilitation and current repairs at the mayoralty office of Urziceni, Satu Mare county	Urziceni Local Council	Project submitted at MDRAPFE to be funded from PNDL II. The funding was not secured. The funding request has been submitted to LEADER
Sanitary sewer system and wastewater treatment plant in the localities of Boghiş, Paulian, Dacia and Traian, part of Doba commune	Doba Local Council	A funding request has been submitted at MDRAPFE to be funded by PNDL. It was not approved
Building the sewerage system for rainwater in the commune of Foieni i	Foieni Local Council	Submitted on PNDL II

(continued)

Table 3.4 (continued)

Project title	Applicant	Achievements after nine months
Sewerage network, including pipe connections and wastewater treatment plant, in the commune of Medieşu Aurit, locality of Iojib	Medieşu Aurit Local Council	Request submitted for funding from PNDL II. Not included in funding due to lack of enough funds
Extending the water network in the locality of Oraşu Nou	Oraşu Nou Local Council	Achieved in 80% from provisioned funds, proposed for funding from PNDL
Sewage in the localities of Hodişa, Cuţa Stan, Socond commune	Socond Local Council	Project submitted at MDRAPFE to be funded from PNDL II. It has not been approved
Establishing a sewage system in the locality of Urziceni Pădure, Urziceni commune, connected at the sewage network from the locality of Urziceni, Satu Mare county	Urziceni Local Council	Project submitted at MDRAPFE to be funded from PNDL II. Rejected. Lack of funds
Extending the electric network from streets Gării, Stadionului, Castanului, Stejarului, Noroieni, Botiz commune	Botiz Local Council	Project submitted to PNDL II—Greater efficiency for public lighting, declared eligible for funding except for street Stejarului and Gării
Greater energy efficiency of public lighting in the commune of Local Council Călineşti Oaş	Călineşti Oaş Local Council	Project submitted to MDRAPFE to be funded from PNDL II. Not approved
Rehabilitation and upgrading of local roads in Pir commune	Pir Local Council	Funding request submitted for PNDL II, waiting for an answer. No funding secured
Rehabilitation of public lighting system in Turulung commune, Satu Mare county	Turulung Local Council	Project proposal. It has been submitted for funding from PNDL II. It has not been approved
Upgrading of 1865 km of communal roads from Bixad commune	Bixad Local Council	Document submitted for funding from PNDL. It has not been approved
Upgrading local interest streets in Căpleni commune	Căpleni Local Council	Submitted to PNDL II. It has not been approved. The project started from its own funds
Upgrading streets and art works in Cehal commune, Satu Mare	Cehal Local Council	Project proposal submitted to MDRAPFE to be funded from PNDL II. It has not been approved
Construction of cycle routes in Certeze commune	Certeze Local Council	Project submitted for funding from PNDL II. It has not been approved

[a] National Company for Investments

submitted projects include various local development problems, from 'enhancing the value of historical monuments', improving buildings' energy efficiency, sewage, water, sewerage systems to construction of cycle routes. This means that only some of them have been directly related to the investment objectives of PNDL II as provisioned in the previously mentioned steps for allocating PNDL II funds. In addition, only some project proposals have explicitly stated the lack of funds for projects that have not been approved. The excerpts selected in the table below also include the case of a project that has only been partially approved—two streets have been excluded in the project, as is the case with Botiz Local Council. Some of the projects submitted for funding for PNDL II have already been submitted for funding to other funding opportunities, like LEADER, from the National Rural Development Program or 'started from own funds' (like in the case of Căpleni Local Council). Simultaneously, not all project proposals submitted for funding for PNDL II have a clear status, although there has been only one session for funding from PNDL II, in relation to the time this report activity has been issued (2017). Still, despite these spots of missing information, this is an example of report which assembles relevant information on project proposals submitted by local public authorities. It offers a good perspective on the project contracted or submitted/ drafted at the level of each territorial administrative unit in the county.

A similar example can be found in the case of Caraş-Severin county.[22] The status of projects published for the moment of July 2018 includes successful projects, irrespective of the source of funding, including draft project proposals submitted by local public authorities, but which still are in the course of evaluation. In this respect, in this latter category lie two project proposals from the municipality of Zorlenţu Mare on sewerage and road infrastructure. They would be funded through 'redistribution of funds from PNDL'.

To conclude, transparent submission and evaluation procedures, as well as a transparent list of submitted projects and their corresponding status (approved, rejected, in the course of evaluation) would significantly improve program transparency. In terms of principal-agent theory, it would also reduce asymmetric information, in the form of hidden action and hidden information, between the principal and agents and, most likely, contribute to an improved perception on the status of open and transparent governance in Romania. It would act, as already stated, as proof of the 'application of law equally to all regardless of their position' (Kyriacou and Roca-Sagales, 2018). The next section provides more insights into the theoretical framework used by the study.

[22] Available at: https://cs.prefectura.mai.gov.ro/wp-content/uploads/sites/33/2018/08/ilovepdf_merged.pdf (date of access: September 6, 2020).

Chapter 4
PNDL at the Crossroads Between Sociology, Public Management and Public Finance: Towards a Theoretical Approach

This study is about public organisations acting in a complex funding environment. Therefore, we draw on concepts and explanatory models from sociology, public management and public finance. Similar to other social science disciplines, there is also diversity within public administration as a field of study. A recent work on this concludes that nowadays public administration is placed at a crossroads, facing serious challenges between its diverse shades as a 'vertical' department in the university hierarchy and a 'horizontal' field with various cross-cutting academic organisational structures and boundaries (Hustedt et al., 2020, 128).

There is diversity within public organisations, within the funding environment and between public organisations and their funding environment. Consequently, this section is divided between a short literature review on characteristics of public organisations, characteristics of funding environment, as well as on the relationships between public organisations and funding environment.

4.1 Characteristics of Public Organisations

Within the view of this study, there are at least six types of organisations: central authorities (represented by the Ministries and the Parliament) and local public authorities—county councils and mayoralties of municipalities, towns and communes, alongside intercommunity development associations (as partnership between public organisations). The section on Study Context presents, in the sub-section on an overview of public administration, indicators related to the relationships between central and local public authorities.

There are certain characteristics of public organisations, as opposed to the private ones: (1) they have publicly elected leaders; (2) they are multifunctional (which implies control problems, representativeness and participation, transparency, equal treatment and quality of services and (3) are not operating in a free and competitive market (Christensen et al., 2007, 6). In this respect, there is, however, a difference

A. M. Marin, *Assessing PNDL*, https://doi.org/10.1007/978-3-030-82844-8_4

between election systems for the two local public organisations included in this study. The President of the County Council is elected from among the elected county councillors, whereas the mayor is directly elected by the people. It means that the mayor can have a political affiliation different from the one of the majority of local councillors. In contrast, this situation is unlikely to happen in the case of the President of the County Council.

In contrast, leaders of other public organisations like the Ministry allocating PNDL II funds are part of the Government and are usually represented by political appointees. Both types of public organisations share common characteristics—are formal organisations, established to serve collective interests and provide specific services (Christensen et al., 2007, 9). Nevertheless, it is worth mentioning that there is a high turnover of the head of Ministries in Romania. The most recent Government change took place in November 2019, and it changed the ruling party (PSD) by the time the funds from PNDL II have been allocated to a minority Government represented by members from the former opposition party (PNL). The Ministry allocating the funds—Ministry of Regional Development and Public Administration has changed not only its head (from a PSD member to a PNL member) but also its name—Ministry of Public Works, Development and Administration.[1] Within this Ministry, there are at least four departments/directions/institutions managing funds allocated to the local public authority: (1) Directorate for Regional Operational Program (EU funds); (2) General Directorate for European Territorial Cooperation (EU funds); (3) Directorate for National Programs Investments in Infrastructure, Constructions and Rehabilitations (with PNDL Compartment) and (4) National Company for Investments in Infrastructure, Constructions and Rehabilitations, under the authority of the same Ministry (State Budget funds—National Program for Investments in Buildings of Public or Social Interest, PNCIPS).

Boundaries between public and private organisations tend to be diffuse. Public organisations are more in the 'grey' area, mostly in a cross-sectorial intersection. The tendency to embrace New Public Management principles has, in fact, made more diffuse these boundaries, while promoting the idea of sub-contracting public services to private or non-profit organisations (Hood, 1995; Hughes, 2003). Partners of public organisations can be private consultancy firms that offer their expertise to draft the necessary documentation for projects.

Furthermore, on the importance of sociology[2] in enhancing the perspective on public organisations, there is a recent plea towards reconnecting sociology and public administration (Bezes, 2020). In this respect, there are four distinct approaches mentioned with various analytical and empirical focus. These are focused on: (1) studying people and individuals; (2) exploring orderings other than political; (3) a world of instruments and organisations in context and (4) bureaucracies as

[1]Organisational structure of the Ministry available at: https://www.mlpda.ro/uploads/articole/attachments/5ecbd73a4df0e817022890.pdf (date of access: June 16, 2020).

[2]Further reference on the added value of sociology in the study of public organisations is available in Kelman (2007).

Table 4.1 Sociological approaches of public bureaucracies

Approaches	Analytical Focus	Empirical focus
Studying people and individuals	Social, educational, gender, ethnic background matter.	Social trajectories Dispositional perspectives Representative bureaucracy Discrimination Gender perspective
Exploring orderings other than political	Beyond politicians vs top bureaucrats Professional, hierarchical, power-based and social dynamics matter within bureaucracies	Professions vs managers Street-level bureaucracies and their discretionary power Ordinary encounters between citizens and bureaucrats
A world of instruments and organisations in context	Critiques of top-down and reified views of bureaucracies; Social and historical constructions of instruments and bureaucratic organisations valuing contexts, uses and practices	Instruments in bureaucracies and in contexts (records, statistics, performance management, rankings, market-based, etc.); Organisational restructuring and redesign of bureaucracies 'Boundary work'
Bureaucracies as institutions	Critique of efficiency → appropriateness Diffusion of rationalised myths and standards. Power struggle between competing actors and competing institutional logics Institutional changes in bureaucracies	Diffusion of organisational formats (mergers, agency); Institutional entrepreneurs in organisational reforms; Trajectories of institutional changes in bureaucracies The many actors of administrative reform processes

Source: Bezes 2020

institutions. The table below details these approaches. Furthermore, in this plea, Bezes (2020) points out that there is also a research agenda in sociology which needs to pay attention to the institutional, context-based and local conditions for the marketisation of public bureaucracies (including the study direction on e-government) (Table 4.1).

In the tension between agency and structure, the managerialist or functionalist perspective places the focus on local governance in providing effective outputs (policies or services) (Denters, 2011). Local authorities presumably have a better knowledge of specific local conditions (genius of place) (Oates, 1999, apud Denters 2011). The democratic perspective emphasises the primacy of popularly elected officials (including local and county councillors) who make the link between community needs and official decisions (ibid.) To put it shortly, local governance rests on two main pillars, differentiated on distinct approaches. The democratic perspective emphasises the role of popularly elected officials, as is the case with directly elected mayors, while the functional perspective emphasises the need to encompass the plenitude of policies and services which the local government performs. Both perspectives face additional challenges when faced with the trend of functional fragmentation, according to the same source (Denters, 2011). In this respect, the cited study refers to the functional fragmentation in the sense of relocation of many traditional local government responsibilities. Yet, for the case of Romania, we could refer to functional fragmentation in both shared responsibilities between local and county local public authorities at agents' level as well as at the principal level, as funding agencies are multiple within the same institution—in our case, Ministry of Regional Development.

Amongst theoretical fields of endeavour, public management is more focused on the manager's role, on its own individual abilities and characteristics, and less on administrative institutions. Key topics are about the relationship between management and rules, structures, resources and context and its effects on public management (Addison, 2009). Managerial capacity equals organisational capacity within this approach (Hou et al., 2003; O'Toole & Meier, 2010, Andrews & Boyne, 2010). The complexity of PNDL analysis is that it takes into account the managers' individual characteristics at two levels of public administration, as president of the county council and mayor of municipality and the interactions between them. The study enlarges the perspective of mayor's managerial abilities as it places them within the context of the county and the managerial abilities of the president of the county council. Therefore, this book is about the individual characteristics in a complex setting of organisations, dependency relations and dynamic environment.

Furthermore, crossroads between levels of organisational analysis can be found alongside micro-macro axis. Examples include the classification provided by Astley and Van de Ven (1983), alongside the institutional theory from Scott (2004), built around regulative, normative and cognitive pillars. The classic organisation theory questions raised by Astley and Van de Ven (1983) are still relevant for reconnecting theoretical boundaries within and outside organisational theories:

- Are organisations functionally rational, technically constrained systems, or socially constructed, subjectively meaningful embodiments of individual action?
- Are changes in organisational forms explained by internal adaptation or by environmental selection?
- Is organisational life determined by intractable environmental constraints, or is it actively created through strategic managerial choices?

- Is the environment to be viewed as a simple aggregation of organisations governed by external economic forces, or as an integrated collectivity of organisations governed by its own internal social and political forces?
- Is organisational behaviour principally concerned with individual or collective action?
- Are organisations neutral technical instruments engineered to achieve a goal, or institutionalised manifestations of the vested interests and power structure of the wider society?

The reconciliation points between the diverging positions mentioned above can be better understood within the framework of systems theory, in which public organisations are viewed as open systems, with influence and influenced by the environment, which is detailed below, in the section on characteristics of funding environment.

4.2 Characteristics of the Funding Environment

A synthetic approach on the conceptualisation of organisational environment is structured alongside three key dimensions: (1) complexity—as complex knowledge required by the environment; (2) lack of stability or dynamism, measured by the rate of changes occurring in the environment and (3) resource availability—as the level of available resources in the environment (Sharfman & Dean, 1991, 683). When seeking an explanatory model for the organisational environment in which local public authorities from Romania operate, it is straightforward that there are different organisational environments for different local public authorities. For instance, urban municipalities under 20,000 are eligible for funding for specific measures from the National Rural Development Plan. In this respect, their resource availability is different from other urban municipalities. Moreover, as mentioned by one of the prominent sources on the topic, there is also a decision of the organisational decision-makers choosing the type of environment in which organisations will operate (Child apud Aldrich, Pfeffer, 1976: 90). Previous studies show that mayors of different levels of territorial administrative units did not enter at all in the competition of European funds for various reasons: passive and risk-averse attitudes, lack of necessary co-funding funds, Eurosceptic political convictions (Dąbrowski, 2010, 310), lack of necessary land registry documents (Marin, 2016). There is also another explanation that might prove to be useful within the context of PNDL II. At the point in time for which this analysis is performed, there are two European funds programming periods. Thus, part of the decisions on 'choosing the environment' might have been based on: (1) the (bad) experiences accumulated up to 2017 in what concerns EU funding—such as slow reimbursement speed, (2) high complexity of the necessary documentation, (3) high turnover of the staff at central and regional levels (intermediate bodies responsible for managing the EU funds at regional level). In this context, there is no surprise that PNDL II seems a more attractive source of funding for at least part of mayors or presidents of the county councils. In particular, the qualitative research conducted for this book provides more insights on the subject.

On this topic, of a particular funding environment over another, early developments from stakeholder analysis might prove useful. In this respect, another review of this theoretical corpus mentions Linderberg's contribution on analysing position and importance of different actors, with a conversion of a previous statement on politics as follows: 'What Do I Want? Who Has It? and When and How Can I Get It?' (Linderberg, 1981 apud Brugha, Varvaszovski, 2020). According to the same source, this early analysis includes an inventory of actors with a role in decision-making, gathering information on them and their importance (accompanied by an appraisal of their importance) and potential for developing alliances (Brugha, Varvaszovski, 2020: 241). Consequently, it looks like a strategy formulation from the perspective of public institutions' leaders. In Romania's case, the law on local public administration (no. 215/2001) states that mayors are the ones responsible for drafting the projects of strategies concerning economic, social and environmental state of the territorial administrative units. These strategic drafts are submitted for approval to the local council. The first programming period even included European funds for increasing local public administration's capacity for strategy formulation—Development of Administrative Capacity Operational Development. Subsequently, part of the local development strategies has been developed with the support of European funds as distinct projects. Nevertheless, local development strategy as a planning process usually takes into account all the funding opportunities, State Budget and European funded, depending on the identification of the local development needs.

Further on, in a systematic review of the relationship between organisations and environment, conducted 'in the most influential general management journals', the surprising finding is that most research published is focused on explaining environmental outcomes rather than organisations (Bansal & Gao, 2006). In this respect, this study is not placed alongside the mainstream of organisations and environment research, as it is centred on explaining organisational outputs/outcomes in the interplay with the environment, whereas the environment is regarded as the context or an explanatory variable. Furthermore, related to another finding of the systematic review, it results that this study is in line with the cross-level[3] analysis as a characteristic of the organisations and environment research. It addresses the individual, organisational and organisational field levels.

Within the funding environment, there are multiple funding lines with similar investment objectives like PNDL II. This topic is presented in the sub-section on the Context of State Budget funded programs. To sum up, for this study, the larger environment is that of the State Budget funds in which multiple layers and various organisations interact: ministries, departments within ministries, county councils

[3]There are five levels of analysis included in the review. These are industrial/institutional, organisational, individual cross-level, and superordinate paradigm (Bansal & Gao, 2006, 467).

and Presidents of County councils, mayors (and local councils). Whereas there are no formal hierarchical relationships between them, it is worth mentioning that these institutions are run by leaders with various political affiliations. Further on, county councils are also involved in allocating part of the equalisation funds for the local councils. According to the Law of public finances (no. 273/2006), a share of 20% of the total sum is allocated, by county council decision, for paying the arrears (as a result of not paying the investment or functioning expenditures), for supporting local development programs or infrastructure projects requiring local co-funding (like PNDL or European-funded projects). County Council Decision in this respect is communicated to the Director of County Directorate of Public Finances, Prefecture and all the local councils in the county. The rest of the sum (meaning 80% of the equalisation funds) is allocated according to a formula computed and published by County Directorates of Public Finances. Still, at the local level, rural and urban municipalities operate in different funding environments depending mainly on the locality characteristics but also on the partnership they have set with other organisations (similar or different to the ones they have). Furthermore, some of them are eligible to apply on specific European-funded lines as well as State Budget funded lines, while others are not eligible on the same number and type of funding lines.

4.3 Relationships Between Public Organisations and Funding Environment

The relationships between public organisations and their funding environment depend on characteristics of both public organisations as well as of the funding environment, including organisations' leadership, but also on the multiple facets of local autonomy (at county and locality level), as previously mentioned about legal autonomy, organisational autonomy, policy scope, effective political discretion, financial autonomy and vertical influence. Characteristics of the funding environment have been outlined in the previous section. All of them can prove to be relevant factors in the relationship between public organisations and funding environment. Yet, organisations are not passive recipients of environmental influences but also have the power to set or contribute to the characteristics of the environment. Especially organisations with high autonomy are able to shape the environment. In particular, in our case, different departments from the same larger public organisation (Ministry of Regional Development and Public Administration) set the conditions for various funding lines: PNDL—first or second phase, the program run by the National Company for Investments or European-funded programs—structural funds or funds for territorial cooperation.

We now turn to focus on the discussion about principal-agent theory, which has been previously used in the study of public finance or public administration. This type of theoretical development has been previously used in the study of design and effectiveness of targeted expenditure programs (Ahmad, Martinez, 2004), public expenditure management systems (Leruth & Paul, 2006), role of mediators between various levels of public administration (de Oliveria & Filho Fontes, 2017) or policy implementation and public policy-making (Lane, 2013), to name but a few. The key reason for including this body of knowledge is represented by the main output of this quest for funds—projects/contracts concluded between two distinct public organisations. Although in the public sector the contractual relationship is set up mainly between agents subordinated to the principal, this is not the case for PNDL. In our model, the Ministry of Regional Development and Public Administration (MDRAP) acts as the principal, providing funds to local authorities (acting as agents) to implement funding objectives as stated in the approved contracts. Within this study, the agents are represented by both county councils as well as mayoralties. The relationship between the Ministry and the local authorities is an agency problem influenced by asymmetric information both in the application as well as in the selection process. Hence, we are not interested in the level of output provided by the agents in order to deliver the highest quality output, but rather in the processes involved in the funds' allocation as well as the outputs derived from this process—contracts, investment objectives and volumes of allocated funds. Problems arising from asymmetric information (hidden action and hidden information) rest with both the principal as well as with the agents. The principal-agent theory states that the agent has better knowledge of the costs of services as it is directly involved in the provision of services, which is not the case for the principal. This information gap might further be used by the agents (if costs are actually lower than the principal envisages). The corresponding conclusion is that 'because of information asymmetry, the agent obtains excess funding to pursue other objectives beyond the knowledge of the principal' (Smith & Bertozzi, 1988, 328). This theory has also been used to conceptualise the engagement of agents in illegal activities such as patronage, corruption, tax evasion, kickbacks and commissions on public contracts (Lane 2013, 87; Leruth & Paul 2006, 4). One of the counter-balance to this situation would be an organisational environment that would be characterised by the rule of law, meaning: (1) predictability, (2) transparency, (3) due process of law, (4) immunities, (5) counter weighing powers, (6) separation of powers and (7) fairness (Lane, 2013, 88), or to put it shortly 'application of law equally to all regardless of their position' (Kyriacou & Roca-Sagales, 2018). The same idea on the importance of good governance in the efficient allocation of public resources is to be found in a recent study on decentralisation and governance in Europe (Kyriacou & Roca-Sagales, 2018). The link between good governance and allocation of EU funds or in general public procurement operations is also underlined in previous studies, in particular in CEE countries (Fazekas, 2014; Doroftei & Dimulescu, 2015). Under the same general concept, countries like Bulgaria, Romania and Croatia score low on this indicator while the Netherlands, Germany and Nordic countries score high.

There are four sets of agency problems related to the principal-agent theory, namely: differences in motivation and goals, informational asymmetries already discussed, different risk propensities and different planning horizons (Smith, Bertozzi, 1998, de Oliveria & Filho Fontes 2017). All these differences are built around the key concept of the theory that is the contract between the party that delegates the activities (the principal) and the one that executes them (the agent). Differences in goals arise from the fact that both parties are trying to maximise their primary utility function (Lane et al., 1998). If we consider the relationship between the principal and the agent as a process variable, then the four sets of problems mentioned above can arise at any moment in time, meaning both ex-ante and ex-post compared to the validity period of the contract.

Moreover, there are also differences in risk preferences which might be related to the type of projects the agents are mostly willing to perform. There are arguments within this theory that the agents prefer actions (or in our terms, projects or investment objectives) that bring results in the short term, a type of behaviour called 'behaviour of managerial myopia' Guimarães dos Santos (2015). This argument can be considered valid in general for the type of projects mayors would like to perform, in the sense that physical investments in particular in roads and water and sewerage are particularly willing to produce visible results in the short term. This finding can be further related to another type of contract within the agency theory, that is between the politicians (both mayors and presidents of the county councils fall in this category) and voters/population.[4] Projects that address the complex needs of marginalised communities or are about investments in educational programs such as school/after school, can be grouped under the ones producing results in the long run and therefore not in the 'top first' preferences of the agents. Nevertheless, agents are willing to apply for a set of investment objectives as considered eligible by the agents. This is why some of the inefficiencies in both public expenditure management as well as in more general, implementation of public policies, should be attributed to the poor program design as conducted by the principal. In this respect, one of the most eloquent examples is the poor programming quality carried out in the previous programming period for a European-funded operational program—POSDRU (Sectoral Operational Program for Development of Human Resources), which has resulted in several infringements for Romania.

Przeworski considers three types of agency relationships: state and private economic agents, citizens and politicians and politicians and public apparatus or bureaucracy (Przeworski, 2003 apud de Oliveria, Filho, Fontes, 2017). For instance, in the relationship between citizens and politicians, studies have been made on cases of clientelism as 'a form of political bargaining that involves exchanges between politicians and citizens where political support is traded for goods and services' (Salazar Dominguez, 2010, 57). Under this perspective, it is useful to mention the distinction between (1) allocation of resources towards provision of public goods; (2) allocations of resources to regions or localities (local public goods) and (3) the case of clientelism, where private goods are allocated to individuals or well-defined sectors of society (Diaz-Cayeros & Magaloni, 2003). Our analysis is focused on local public goods at the county and municipality level. We study the relationship

[4]The relationship has been viewed as a contract between the voters as principal and the state (or municipality, county council, Parliament, etc.) as the agent.

between different parties of the state, from central to local public administration, with politicians and bureaucrats involved at all levels. In return for other types of resource allocations (not necessarily only for PNDL II), there have been cases where political bargaining involving politicians resulted in changes in political affiliation. Still, even if there are clear differences between clientelism (based on the allocations of private goods) and allocations for producing local public goods, both are related to transparent budgetary mechanisms and good governance in general.

A further theoretical distinction needs to be mentioned here, that of interdependency relationships. This theme draws on the resource dependency theory, developed by Pfeffer and Salancik (1978), as a way to analyse the relationship between the organisation and the environment at the level of interorganisational network. There are several types of interdependencies based on the power relationships, results (outcomes) and organisational behaviour, as follows: (1) symmetric interdependencies (balanced power relationships) and asymmetric, further differentiated in (2) results dependencies (which is a product of two or more systems) and (3) behaviour dependencies (activities for one system are linked with another system). In addition, results dependencies can be competitive (results for one system are achieved at the expense of another system) and symbiotic (results for one system is a result for another or two systems are reciprocally dependent on each other's result) (Marion, 1999). Interorganisational dependency depends on: (1) the degree to which a certain resource is used (magnitude of dependency resource); (2) importance or 'power' of a specific resource; (3) the degree to which a certain group has discretionary power over the resource necessary for another group; (4) the degree in which the control of a resource is concentrated. The analysis of key stakeholders is viewed as a way to integrate resource–dependence and institutional theories in the organisational analysis (Gomes, 2006, 80). In our case, we can identify the control of financial resources as well as the legal prerogatives for managing the implementation of the State Budget funded programs as sources of power for MDRAP over the local communities. The degree to which the local communities depend on the principal's power can be measured by their fiscal capacity, that is the share of own autonomous revenues in the total local budget revenues. This brings back the issue of financial autonomy previously mentioned. At the same time, the availability of the financial resources needs to be analysed in the larger context of the organisation's environment, including the availability of European funds for the same funding objectives. To add even more complexity to the stakeholders/environmental analysis for this study, there are also power relationships between the county councils and local municipalities. Part of them results from the legislation as the equalisation formula stipulated in the Law on local public finances (Law no. 273/2006) has been several times changed through the Annual Budget Laws. The year which left maximum discretion in the allocation criteria is 2008 when the entire sum has been allocated by County Council decision for all the territorial administrative units within the county (Art. 6, letter d, State Budget Law for 2008, no. 388/2007).

Within the relationship between the organisations and the environment, some organisational characteristics tend to be spread throughout other units/organisations facing the same environmental contexts, a process that has been called isomorphism. DiMaggio and Powell's (1983) seminal work on institutional isomorphism distinguishes between (1) coercive isomorphism related to political influence and the problem of legitimacy; (2) mimetic isomorphism in response to uncertainty and (3) normative isomorphism, related to professionalisation. Their work also advances a hypothesis that might prove useful for this paper—'the greater the extent to which an organisational field is dependent upon a single (or several similar) source of support for vital resources, the higher the level of isomorphism' (p. 155) or 'the greater the extent of structuration of a field, the greater the amount of institutional isomorphic change' (p. 156).

For the individual level, within the organisational context, a useful concept is that of adaptive leadership, defined as 'an interactive event in which knowledge, action preferences and behaviours change, thereby provoking an organisation to become more adaptive' (Lichtenstein et al., 2006, 4). Its utility for this research resides in the usage of complexity theory in the study of leadership, which is conceived as a complex adaptive system phenomenon, in which interactions between agents play a key role, and leadership is a process (rather than an individual) conceived as an emergent event (ibid.). It thus reinforces the idea of the subjective meanings of the environment created by individuals through interactions in a dynamic, evolving process leading to complex adaptive systems.

Further on the individual level, that of organisation's leadership, another comparative survey at the European level focuses on political leaders at a local level, namely mayors and local councillors. Its most recent results are collected in a book on the European Mayor—(Heinelt et al., 2018). It examines various aspects related to local politics, among which there are references related to the mayors' institutional environment, social background, political career, perceptions, leadership styles, entrepreneurialism, political leadership, vertical relations, relations and conflict among municipal actors, administrative reform and spatial planning. The latest survey on mayors conducted in 2014–2016 is part of the surveys starting in 1995 as an initiative of individual members of the standing groups on Local Government and Politics of the European Consortium of Political Research and/or the European Urban Research Association. Romania has been represented in only one survey of councillors (at the second tier of local government) conducted in 2012–2013.[5] For the purpose of this study, it is useful to mention the analysis of the institutional environment in which mayors act. Their analysis considers both horizontal and vertical power relations. Horizontal relations refer to the relationships between the mayor, the council and the municipal administration, and vertical relations relate to the relation and competencies and control of the local level within the political multi-level system of a country (Heinelt et al., 2018: 20). These dimensions, among others, are also considered for refining typologies of local government systems for Eastern Europe in order to differentiate between country variations more clearly (Swianiewicz, 2014). More precisely, this tailor-made typology for

[5] Volume of the sample N=177 (Heinelt and Magnier, 2018, 162).

the municipalities in countries in the part of Europe where Romania lies considers the following:

- Territorial organisation, considering two indicators: (1) number of tiers of elected local and regional governments (only tiers of both elected representatives and locally appointed are accounted for) and (2) territorial fragmentation, as the average population size of municipal government unit.
- Functional decentralisation—share of sub-national expenditures in GDP.
- Financial discretion of local governments, measured by three variables: (1) financial decentralisation—share of locally controlled taxes (that can be directly influenced by local governments) in total revenues; (2) the shape of the grant allocation system as 'traditionally, grant allocation was one of the most important means for exercising power and control by the higher tiers towards lower tiers of government' (Swianiewicz, 2014, 302); and (3) local government debt as a percentage of GDP in the sense of measuring in direct correlation the local fiscal autonomy (ibid.)
- Horizontal power relations relate to (1) the position of the mayor in the municipal government and (2) the electoral system of the local council (majoritarian, proportional or mixed).

According to the dimensions considered by the typology, Romania is part of a group of the so-called Balkan countries, together with Albania, Bulgaria, Croatia, Macedonia, Moldova, Slovenia and Ukraine. Their common features are represented by the direct election of mayors. Yet, the scope of local government functions is much narrow than that present in the countries labelled as 'champions of decentralisation' (Hungary, Poland and Slovakia) and type II, 'relatively decentralised'[6] (Czech Republic, Estonia and Latvia).

Accountability mechanisms for projects funded by European funds are, in general, strong in particular in terms of the formal procedures concerned. There is, however, a distinction between the layers of the analysis involved—that of the organisation and that of political actors involved. In this respect, there is an asymmetry of accountability, meaning there is an unequal distribution of accountability between actors. This is further translated in the fact that 'political representatives are still able to act highly ineffectively and uneconomically without bringing down unwanted consequences upon themselves' (Vesely, 2013, 318). Related to accountability mechanisms for EU funded projects, shares of the volumes of funds implemented are subject to accountability mechanisms, yet there is a whole system 'where it is relatively easy to spend (or even steal) billions from the public budget' (Vesely, 2013, 319). Yet, for the case of local public organisations like urban and rural municipalities, this part of accountability mechanisms mainly refers to the implementation phase of projects rather than the selection phase. On

[6]The key difference between type I (champions of decentralisation) is the small share of locally controlled taxes (Swianiewicz, 2014, 305). Further references on the characteristics of public administration in Romania in the European context in Thijs et al. (2018b).

the contrary, if we refer to the central public administration managing the funds, the principal—Ministry of Regional Development and Public Administration, then there should be accountability mechanisms involved in the budgetary execution (including allocation of funds) of the State Budget funded programs, like the one analysed by the present study, National Local Development Program. Yet, this type of accountability depends on the power of control institutions (such as the Romanian Court of Accounts) or on the internal monitoring and evaluation mechanisms, which are in their turn, dependent on the initial (poor) program design.

In line with all of the factors mentioned above, the explanatory model for funds allocated at the local levels from PNDL includes variables related to multiple layers:

- county level—President of the County Council's political affiliation and experience (more than 10 years in the position of the President of the County Council), number of competitors in the organisational field (number of territorial administrative units in the respective county)
- regional level—localisation within a specific development region which is more likely to absorb most part of the corresponding funds
- local level—mayor's political affiliation, municipality's fiscal capacity, experience with the new programming period of Structural Funds (2014–2020), results of the absorption capacity of European funds in the previous programming period, participation in a Local Action Group in accordance with the rules for the new National Rural Development Program, municipality's population size, area, density of the population
- individual leadership/managerial level—mayor's political affiliation, president of the county council's political affiliation and experience (more than 10 years in the position of the President of the County Council).

To sum up, there are multiple faceted elements acting in different funding environments for various territorial administrative units in Romania. The next sections explore them while presenting in a detailed picture the 'outputs' of the quest for State Budget funds.

Chapter 5
Key Findings

5.1 General Results

At first glance, getting funds for the local community from PNDL II would mean a typical process in which a mayoralty (usually not in partnership for this funding line) drafts a project based on the local needs, submits it to the Ministry and, depending on the selection criteria or procedure, gets the funding. Nevertheless, the funded projects depend on the total limit allocated through State Budget Law, which is sometimes approved after the deadline of receiving the proposals. MPs can also amend this law with specific investment objectives, although in practice, their amendments have not been approved. Furthermore, the proposed investment objective can be approved for funding and included in the corresponding ministerial order issued, but the funding contract between the Ministry and the territorial administrative unit can last longer. In the previous session (PNDL I), a part of the contracts from Maramureş county has not been signed in the year 2014, thus exceeding the provisioned term of 2014. Correspondingly, the sums could not be used in the fiscal year of 2014. In the qualitative research conducted for this study, for the case of PNDL II, one mayor from a rural community mentioned the case of 'an interrupted communication until the funding contract has been signed'.

> At the beginning, there were some hindrances. At that time, I have been very disappointed that we are not signing the projects, everybody around us succeeded in signing, but we didn't. Yet, we were there, among the approved projects, but nobody asked us to sign the contract, I think it took us some time until the contract has been signed. Communication was somehow broken in the beginning, we asked, we requested supplementary explanations, but nobody gave us any explanation. (Mayoralty representative, South development region)

Data analysis at a national level shows that the highest mean value for PNDL allocations (in euro/inhabitant) is registered for the territorial administrative units with the largest share from this stage of allocations from PNDL II. More than two thirds of the funds have been allocated to municipalities from rural area (Fig. 5.1). These are the rural municipalities for which there is also the largest dispersion of distribution (Table 5.1). The highest minimum levels of allocations

A. M. Marin, *Assessing PNDL*, https://doi.org/10.1007/978-3-030-82844-8_5

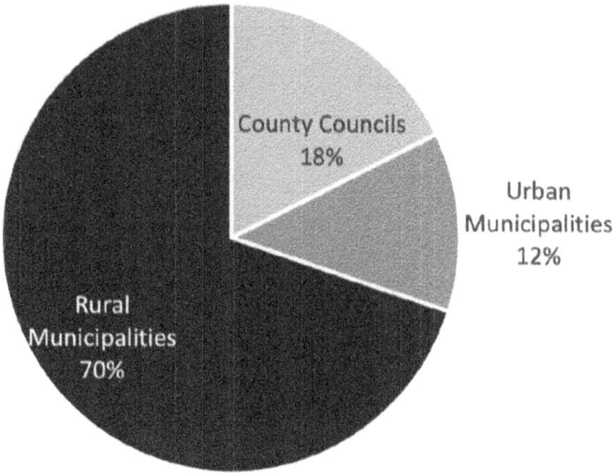

Fig. 5.1 PNDL II allocations by territorial administrative unit. Data: author's calculations based on the database of contracts awarded under PNDL 2017–2020. The sums computed for each level (county councils, urban and rural municipalities) represent allocations in lei, not transformed into euro/inhabitant

(in euro/inhabitant) are for the county councils. As for the largest maximum levels of allocations, these are again for rural municipalities.

The standard deviation of the distribution of allocations for rural municipalities is more than three times larger than for urban municipalities. These large dispersions in the distribution of indicator for all levels of local public administration pose significant challenges for achieving a good explanatory model that would account for a large part of the variance of the dependent variable, PNDL allocations in euro/inhabitant. This is why, as explained in the section on Data and Method, the dependent variables have been used with their logarithmic values, as detailed in the explanatory models corresponding to each section/level of analysis.

5.2 Descriptive Results at the Level of County Councils

If we consider the volume of funds absorbed by each County Council in relation to county's population, the maximum values (in euro/inhabitant) are registered for the counties of Ialomiţa, Neamţ and Vrancea. Yet, there are notable differences between these three counties. The gap between the volume of funds in Ialomiţa and that in Neamţ is a significant one—219.59 euro/inhabitant compared to 147.52 euro/inhabitant. In contrast, minimum values are registered in the counties of Olt, Prahova and Hunedoara (with the lowest value registered in Hunedoara—9.23 euro/inhabitant). In addition, the counties of Alba and Constanţa have not absorbed at all funds from the PNDL II session under analysis in this study (Fig. 5.2). Nevertheless, it is not clear whether they did not apply at all to the program, or if they applied and the submitted projects have not been considered eligible for funding. Official responses received from the Ministry of Regional Development and Public Administration are included in the Annex. The information provided does not distinguish between these possibilities. As already mentioned,

Table 5.1 Descriptive statistics for PNDL II allocations by level of analysis

PNDL allocations (euro/inhabitant)	Number of cases	Mean	Median	Minimum	Maximum	Standard deviation	Variance
County Councils	39	69.54	64.01	9.23	219.59	44.32	1964.369
Municipalities—total	2886	606	424.5	3.11	14,313.48	675.11	455,783.63
Urban municipalities	289	218.10	137.78	3.11	1353.05	220.789	48,748.19
Rural municipalities	2597	648.92	463.87	5.7	14313.48	694.63	482,521.85

Data: Author's calculations based on the database of contracts awarded under PNDL 2017–2020. The descriptive indicators are computed for PNDL allocations aggregated at municipality/county council level, only for those units that received allocations (municipalities/County Councils with zero allocated funding are excluded from this analysis). The indicator refers to PNDL allocations in euro/inhabitant

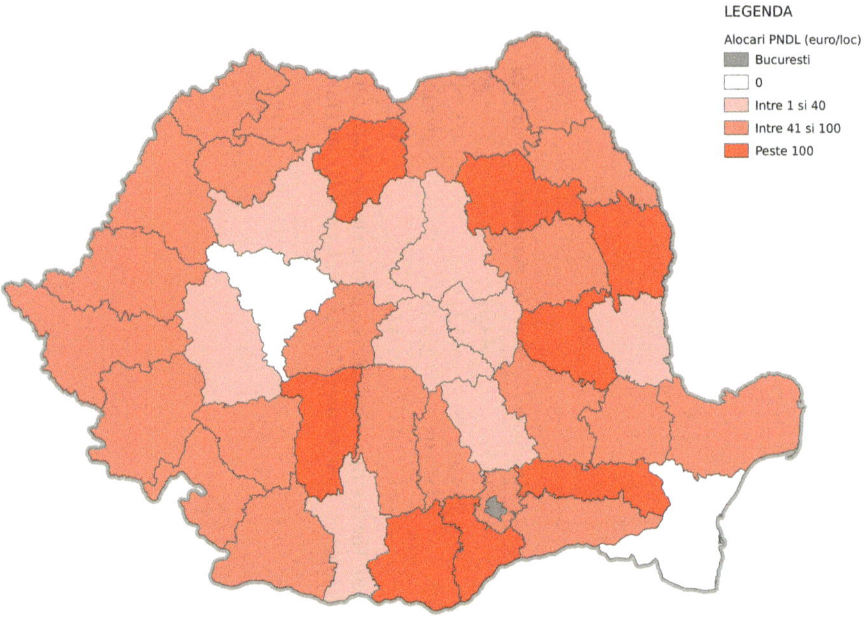

Fig. 5.2 Distribution of PNDL funds at the level of County Councils. Data: author's calculations based on the information in the database of contracts awarded under PNDL 2017–2020. Note: the map presents the distribution of funds for county councils (as euro/inhabitant), not for the entire county

the Ministry considers that project proposals received by them are not considered public information under their responsibility, although such public information has been previously published by other contracting authorities—such as the Ministry of Agriculture and Rural Development in the past programming period. According to the same response, the Ministry considers information concerning projects submission as public only if the request is addressed to each public authority (county or municipality).

On average, the volume of funds received by county councils with the same political affiliation as the ruling party (PSD) is higher than that of the rest of the county councils, with a different political affiliation. Yet, this difference is not statistically significant (tested with one way ANOVA). The same finding applies if we also consider the political affiliation of UDMR as a supporter of the ruling party, and therefore, the analysis takes into consideration a higher mean value. In order to further explore this issue, a regression model is included and explained in the next section.

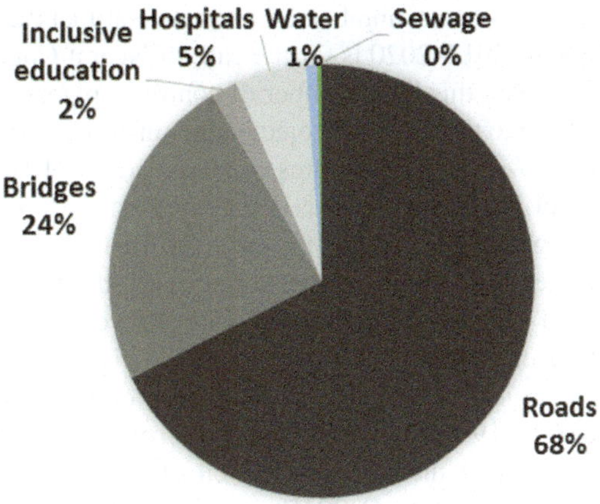

Fig. 5.3 Objectives of PNDL investments (County Councils). Data: author's calculations based on the information in the database of contracts awarded under PNDL 2017–2020. Multiple response, N=346 contracts

5.2.1 *Where Does the Money Go? Contracts and Investment Objectives*

There are a total of 346 contracts allocated for the County Councils within PNDL 2017–2020, stage of implementation as of May 1, 2018. Only four of them have multiple investment objectives, in contrast with the numerous contracts with multiple investment objectives for the projects allocated to the level of municipalities. County roads and bridge infrastructure account for almost all investments objectives (237 contracts for the roads infrastructure and 83 contracts for the bridge infrastructure—Fig. 5.3). Figure 5.3 roads infrastructure projects covered various types of constructions: rehabilitation, upgrading, consolidation, road paving. Only three projects are dedicated to investments in the water and sewerage infrastructure.

Only a few contracts of the County Councils target investments in the social infrastructure, although at the local level, there is a significant part of the social assistance and child protection responsibilities within the subordinated institutions—General Directorates of Social Assistance and Child Protection. Just as a reminder, according to the prioritisation criteria for PNDL II, social infrastructure represents top priority—in the first step, there is a priority for projects focusing on nursery schools and kindergartens, as well as schools without sanitary or emergency authorisation. Notwithstanding, part of these public institutions is also under mayoralties' responsibility. There are some County Councils requesting funds for the health infrastructure (18 contracts). For instance, Cluj County Council received funds for seven projects targeting investments in the health infrastructure, mainly provision of modern equipment.[1] In addition, only seven projects aim the improvement of school infrastructure (inclusive education units or vocational schools).

[1] The other County Councils with projects directed towards health infrastructure are: Arad, Arges, Ialomita, Iasi, Ilfov, Neamt, Satu Mare, Salaj and Sibiu.

The largest number of projects/contracts approved for a County Council for PNDL 2017–2020 is for the case of Neamţ County Council with 57 projects (Table 5.2). Yet, this high number of contracts places Neamţ amongst the last positions in regard to the average project value (in euro). For this indicator, the highest scores are for Buzau and Maramureş counties (around 19 mil euro average value per contract).

In what concerns variations of costs between similar projects, we have taken a closer look only at projects on road infrastructure. Here the published list of projects only includes, in some cases, the length of roads to be upgraded through each project. In this regard, Caraş-Severin County Council represents one of the best examples, as their projects clearly state the number of kilometres included by project, for instance: Upgrading county road 608B, Copăcele-Zorlencior, km 8+600–19+600, length of county road 11.00 km. Following the same pattern, it results that the County Council of Buzău intends to include in one project 24.5 km—Upgrading DJ204C, km 60+000–84+500, county boundary with Vrancea-Bisoca-Săruleşti-Vintilă Vodă, Buzău county. The total value of the project is about 22 mil euro,[2] which means a mean value of about 900,000 euro for one km. The substantiation study conducted by the WB (Marteau et al., 2014, 87–88) mentions a legal provision from 2010 (GD 363/2010), which sets the standard cost for the modernisation of one kilometre of county road at 332,832 euro. Nevertheless, it goes without saying that each project cost should be carefully analysed in the context of provisioned works for each county road. As already pointed out, it could be the case that the agent (Buzau County Council) has better knowledge of the costs of services than the principal (MDRAP) as it is directly involved in the provision of services, yet large differences deserve special attention.

In addition, it is not clear how the needs in terms of road infrastructure are substantiated. Data from the National Institute of Statistics include modernised roads, roads with stone pavement or earth roads, whereas county development strategies use different data on these categories of roads technical status[3] or assess that a large part of the road network has an expired working term of validity.[4] Therefore, for increased program transparency, explicit data sources should be mentioned and included in program guidelines/ selection or prioritisation criteria.

The focus is turned now on the estimated needs for specific investment objectives. In this respect, the report on the status of the territory states that, according to World Bank studies (MDRAP, 2018: 66), the largest investment needs for county roads are located in Iasi, Cluj, Suceava, Argeş, Bacău and Bihor. However, the analysis of PNDL allocations shows different results. If we differentiate among the awarded projects only investments objectives related to county roads and bridges

---

[2]If we take into consideration a medium value of 4.5.

[3]For example, annual Report 2017 of the President of Alba County Council, available at: http://www.cjalba.ro/rapoarte-de-activitate/ (date of access: February 1st, 2019).

[4]For instance, Mures County Council, Territorial Development Infrastructure Strategy for Mures county, Transport Infrastructure. Strategy synthesis (Mures County Council, 2012) http://www.cjmures.ro:1880/urbanism/patj/parte_scrisa/Partea%20III%20vol%20XI%20-%20Strategia.pdf.

Table 5.2 PNDL projects of the County Councils—number, total volume of funds and average PNDL contract value

No	County name	Number of PNDL projects	Total volume of funds absorbed through PNDL (euro)	Average PNDL contract value (euro)
1	ALBA	0	0	0
2	ARAD	5	42,116,814	8,423,363
3	ARGES	9	29,083,522	3,231,502
4	BACAU	8	40,803,658	5,100,457
5	BIHOR	3	41,049,851	13,683,284
6	BISTRITA-NASAUD	12	37,104,397	3,092,033
7	BOTOSANI	7	19,145,991	2,735,142
8	BRAILA	6	13,276,499	2,212,750
9	BRASOV	5	12,868,033	2,573,607
10	BUZAU	2	38,154,107	19,077,054
11	CARAŞ-SEVERIN	7	22,338,735	3,191,248
12	CLUJ	23	16,461,773	715,729.2
13	CONSTANŢA	0	0	0
14	COVASNA	4	3,881,022	970,255.6
15	DAMBOVITA	21	29,969,340	1,427,111
16	DOLJ	4	28,871,710	7,217,927
17	GALATI	1	9,003,364	9,003,364
18	GORJ	2	33,718,338	16,859,169
19	HARGHITA	3	8,157,297	2,719,099
20	HUNEDOARA	1	3,865,375	3,865,375
21	IALOMITA	6	60,198,927	10,033,154
22	IASI	9	38,675,404	4,297,267
23	ILFOV	3	20,956,653	6,985,551
24	MARAMURES	2	37,480,280	18,740,140
25	MEHEDINTI	4	16,988,972	4,247,243
26	MURES	4	12,097,754	3,024,438
27	NEAMT	57	69,446,194	1,218,354
28	OLT	1	5,024,594	5,024,594
29	PRAHOVA	4	8,189,270	2,047,317
30	SALAJ	5	14,116,116	2,823,223
31	SATU MARE	11	30,890,557	2,808,232
32	SIBIU	5	35,883,486	7,176,697
33	SUCEAVA	9	47,494,563	52,77,174
34	TELEORMAN	9	38,818,380	4,313,153
35	TIMIS	10	30,993,099	3,099,310
36	TULCEA	6	12,414,651	2,069,109
37	VALCEA	13	44,820,379	3,447,721
38	VASLUI	17	38,815,524	2,283,266
39	VRANCEA	32	49,295,231	1,540,476
40	CALARASI	3	26,335,210	8,778,403
41	GIURGIU	13	29,300,636	2,253,895

Data: Author's calculations based on the information in the database of contracts awarded under PNDL 2017–2020. Multiple response, N=346 contracts (bridges are located on county roads), top 5 counties include Neamţ, Vrancea, Vaslui, Dâmboviţa, Vâlcea and Bistriţa Năsăud. Therefore, among them, only Neamţ and Vaslui are assessed with medium-high investment needs for county roads.

The Less Transparent, the More Attractive? Volume of Funds: A Comparative Perspective Between PNDL and European Funding

For the minimum level, there are two county councils that did not receive any funds from the program PNDL 2017–2020. These are the County Councils of Alba and Constanţa. Yet, neither of these two councils are placed in the top 10 of county councils in terms of euro/capita absorbed in the period of 2009–2015 from European funds. Among those who received funding, the County Councils of Hunedoara, Prahova and Olt succeeded in absorbing around 10 euro/capita from PNDL II (Table 5.3). Nevertheless, all three of them absorbed a significant volume of European funds, as can be noticed from the same Table.

The example of County Council of Alba might be explained by its development targets set in relation to the European Funding available for the programming period of 2014–2020. In this respect, the County Development Strategy for Alba for the period of 2014–2020[5] includes initiatives regarding elaboration and submission of projects related to:

- Improvement of county/regional health infrastructure—four projects aimed at improving the infrastructure of hospitals, to be submitted with the Regional Development Operational Program 2014–2020, Priority Axis no. 3—Supporting the shift towards a low-carbon economy.
- Improvement of county roads infrastructure, project submitted in partnership[6] with other urban and local authorities for funding through the Regional Development Operational Program 2014—2020.
- Other projects elaborated and implemented in partnership with national and international organisations/institutions, submitted for funding from the Human Capital Operational Program, Regional Development Operational Program or Europe for citizens.

  A similar explanation applies for the County Council of Constanţa, stating in its annual activity report (report of the President of the County Council)[7] that they already succeeded in securing European funding for the following development objectives:

[5] Annual Report 2017 of the President of Alba County Council, available at: http://www.cjalba.ro/rapoarte-de-activitate/ (date of access: February 1st, 2019).

[6] In partnership with the municipality of Aiud and with the communes of Bucium, Mogos, Pogor si Ramet.

[7] Annual Report 2017 of the President of Constanţa County Council, available at: http://www.cjc.ro/dyn_doc/cjc/rapoarte_activitate_consilieri_judeteni/2017-2018/RA_Tutuianu_Marius_Horia_2017-2018.pdf.

Table 5.3 Volume of funds/capita absorbed through European funding and PNDL

No	County name	Total volume of European-funded projects (euro/capita), absorbed in the period of 2009_2017	Total volume of funds absorbed through PNDL (euro/capita)
1	ALBA	86.54	0.00
2	ARAD	112.40	97.80
3	ARGES	57.46	47.49
4	BACAU	112.37	66.22
5	BIHOR	80.44	71.34
6	BISTRITA-NASAUD	231.08	129.63
7	BOTOSANI	194.59	46.40
8	BRASOV	3.43	23.43
9	BRAILA	110.56	41.33
10	BUZAU	82.91	84.59
11	CARAŞ-SEVERIN	122.34	75.58
12	CLUJ	89.51	23.82
13	CONSTANŢA	134.01	.00
14	COVASNA	219.33	18.47
15	DAMBOVITA	81.03	57.77
16	DOLJ	125.76	43.71
17	GALATI	39.93	16.79
18	GORJ	110.70	98.71
19	HARGHITA	183.40	26.24
20	HUNEDOARA	200.78	9.23
21	IALOMITA	20.70	219.59
22	IASI	140.79	50.08
23	ILFOV	107.49	53.91
24	MARAMURES	163.27	78.30
25	MEHEDINTI	325.76	64.02
26	MURES	127.27	21.96
27	NEAMT	133.72	147.52
28	OLT	103.13	11.51
29	PRAHOVA	82.72	10.73
30	SATU MARE	63.84	89.70
31	SALAJ	331.16	62.91
32	SIBIU	147.91	90.31
33	SUCEAVA	140.65	74.82
34	TELEORMAN	152.85	102.12
35	TIMIS	64.81	45.34
36	TULCEA	224.19	58.26
37	VASLUI	131.14	104.42
38	VALCEA	252.30	113.33
39	VRANCEA	138.16	144.85
40	CALARASI	173.45	85.87
41	GIURGIU	190.02	104.12

Data: Author's calculations based on the information in the database of contracts awarded under PNDL 2017–2020. Multiple response, N=346 contracts

- Upgrading of county roads infrastructure, project approved for funding through the Regional Development Operational Program 2014–2020;
- A set of projects submitted for funding in the area of cultural heritage;
- A set of projects submitted for European funding in the area of child protection system;
- Two projects regarding regional transport infrastructure submitted for assessment within the European-funded programs.

For the maximum level, the top 3 of State Budget Funds absorbed through PNDL includes the counties of Ialomiţa, Neamţ and Vrancea. The case of Ialomiţa County Council is of special interest, as detailed below.

One session of funding through PNDL (1 year) represents half or more of all the funding applications in 9 years of European funding, as can be noticed from Table 5.3. Nevertheless, when comparing the volume of funds between these two funding lines, one needs to bear in mind that PNDL 2017–2020 represents only one session of funding, while the same analysis period (2009–2017) also covers another session of PNDL—that of 2015–2019 (not covered in this paper). Therefore, it is likely that in some cases, the total volume of funds absorbed through PNDL might furthermore surpass the volume of European funds from the previous programming period. For most County Councils in Romania, the funds received within PNDL 2017–2020 represent equal to or more than half of the total volume of all European funds received in the period of 2009–2015 (in euro/capita). This means that more than half of the County Councils received a significant volume of funding. Therefore, the Program is highly attractive to the county public authorities. Moreover, there is also a set of 10 County Councils receiving through PNDL more than 80% of the total volume of European funds absorbed in the period of 2009—2015. In this picture, there are two 'outlier' cases worth mentioning: the County Councils of Ialomiţa and Braşov.

In only one session of funding (1 year), through PNDL 2017–2020, Ialomiţa County Council succeeded in absorbing more than ten times the total volume of European funds absorbed throughout a period of nine years (2009–2017)—219.59 euro/capita through PNDL, compared to 20.7 euro/capita through European funds. According to the strategic programming conducted by Ialomiţa County Council, at least part of the county roads should have been rehabilitated/upgraded with the support of European Funds.[8]

In addition, Brasov County Council accomplished a similar success in terms of the difference in volume of funds between the two lines of funding. Still, one needs to take into consideration that, compared to the rest of the County Councils, the volume of funds for Brasov County Council is in the lower category—both for the European funds, as well as for the examined State Budget funds. Additionally, absorption of EU or State Budget funds should be viewed as a process variable. This

[8]Source: Ialomita County Council, Development Strategy of Ialomita county 2009–2020, Chapter VII, Priority Project Fiches, available at: http://cjialomita.ro/despre-noi/programe-si-strategii/strategia-de-dezvoltare-a-judetului-ialomita/# (date of access: February 1, 2019).

picture only captures the situation for the year 2018, with absorption of EU funds until 2017 and absorption of PNDL II funds awarded in 2018.

Another interesting example is at the opposite end of the scale, that of the 'champions' of European funding. For instance, the County Council of Hunedoara succeeded in absorbing 201 euro/capita[9] from the European funds and only 9.23 euro from PNDL.

Here, there is a need to make an additional remark. The marked differences between EU and State Budget funding have also been mentioned by the participants in the qualitative research, as detailed in the next sections. Furthermore, differences between the two funding lines have been put under the spotlight when the Government tried to settle the expenditures from PNDL (in 2019) by funding them from EU funds (Large Infrastructure Operational Program). This attempt took the form of an amendment submitted to be adopted in the Parliament as a legislative project for approving Government Emergency Ordinance no. 30/2018 on setting some measures in the field of European funds and for completing some legal draft legislation.[10] Nevertheless, this proposal of the Romanian Government has not been approved by the European Commission, DG Regio. On this topic, Fiscal Council (2020) has warned that the request of the Romanian Government to settle post-factum reimbursements from PNDL will not be approved. Most likely, according to the press releases,[11] this has been related to the differences in rules and general strategic approach.

To conclude, from all the information mentioned above, it seems that, at least for a part of County Councils, there is a case of behaviour dependency. This mean that, examining in a comparative perspective the funding environments of EU funds and State Budget funds, activities for one system are linked with another system. If we consider only the perspective of the principal (represented by Ministries), results dependencies are compulsory, in the sense that all approved projects should avoid double funding for the same investment objective. Yet, if we change the perspective at the agents' level, the situation could turn up to be different. In other words, under the theoretical distinction in reference to the relationships between public organisations and funding environment, it could be the case that results are competitive, in the sense that results for one system are achieved at the expense of another system. The recommended approach would be that these results are symbiotic, namely two systems are reciprocally dependent on each other's result (Marion, 1999). A subsequent discussion would be what result means, if we only

[9]Placed among the 'top 10' county councils of European funding.

[10]Transcripts of the meeting in the Parliament are available here, including the suggestion from MDRAP representative to use EU funds for funding PNDL projects: http://www.cdep.ro/pls/steno/steno2015.stenograma?ids=7975&idm=8 (date of access: September 3, 2020).

[11]See, for instance, https://www.g4media.ro/exclusiv-comisia-europeana-a-refuzat-o-gaselnita-a-guvernului-dancila-care-voia-sa-deconteze-din-fonduri-ue-proiectele-de-apa-si-canalizare-date-baronilor-psd-prin-celebrul-pndl.html or https://www.digi24.ro/stiri/economie/business-club-pndl-facut-varza-de-bruxelles-guvernul-dancila-primeste-o-lovitura-financiara-de-la-comisia-europeana-1204455 (date of access: September 3, 2020).

refer to successful project application or to the process of applying in itself. In our view, the entire system should have a coherent coordination offering prospects for development for every locality while ensuring the rule of law in project application, selection, implementation and monitoring and evaluation. In order to have an extended view on this, the next section examines the role of the volume of EU funds within an explanatory model based on a multiple regression analysis.

5.2.2 A Closer Look: A Typology of the County Councils by Type and Volume of Funds

This section combines results achieved in two different funding environments in order to build a typology of the County Councils. To sum up, there are three dimensions considered for developing a typology of the county councils in respect to the volume of funds absorbed through PNDL (Table 5.4). Table 5.4, the typology is based on the view on funds' absorption as a process, and it combines funding lines as well as programming/allocation phases for both European and State Budget funds. Through this mixture of funding lines, past and current, the results are as follows:

1. Winners of PNDL—upper quartile of the total volume of funds absorbed through PNDL
2. Winners of European funding (previous programming period)—upper quartile of the total volume of funds absorbed through European funding (2007–2013)
3. Winners of current EU funding—binary variable on whether the county councils succeeded in the current programming period to have EU funded projects in implementation. This variable is operationalised through whether they reported or not expenditures in the local budgets execution Annex no. 24 (budgetary code 58: Projects with funding from external no reimbursable funds for the financial framework 2014–2020).

Using these three dimensions, the results can be grouped under the following categories:

- 'Losing it all'. These county councils have not yet started implementing European-funded projects in the current programming period and are not placed in the upper quartiles of volume of absorbed funds neither for the European funding nor for PNDL. Yet, this does not mean that they have not succeeded in absorbing funds at all; it should only be interpreted that they are not among the 'winners' for the analysed funding lines. These are the county councils of Bacău, Braşov, Dâmboviţa, Mureş, Olt, Sibiu and Timiş.
- 'Living in the Past'. These are county councils that succeeded in absorbing a significant volume of European funding in the last programming period; however, they did not manage to have other EU projects at present time and also are not

Table 5.4 Categories of county councils

European-funded projects in implementation in the current programming period (2014–2020)			Winners of European funds from the last programming period		Total
			No	Yes	
No	PNDL winners	No	Underachievers, 'Losing it all' 7 CC	'Living in the Past' (previous programming EU winners) 3 CC	10
		Yes	State Budget winners (PNDL winners) 5	0	5
Yes	PNDL winners	No	EU is the present (current programming EU winners) 17 CC	Past and present EU winners 4 CC	21
		Yes	Mix and match—present mixed funding approach 2 CC	All times winners (EU current and past as well as PNDL winners) 3 CC	5
Total			31	10	41

Data: Author's calculations based on the information in the database of contracts awarded under PNDL 2017–2020 as well as budgetary information on EU funds

placed among the top winners of PNDL funding (upper quartile). These are the counties of Botoşani, Covasna and Hunedoara.

- National funding is the best (State Budget Winners). This case is one of the most interesting types for the purpose of this analysis as it is primarily targeting State Budget funds in the form of PNDL program. They are not among the winners of the past or current funding opportunities offered by EU funds. These are the counties of Ialomiţa, Neamţ, Teleorman, Vaslui and Vrancea.
- EU is the present—Alba, Argeş, Bihor, Brăila, Buzău, Caraş-Severin, Cluj, Constanţa, Dolj, Galaţi, Harghita, Iaşi, Ilfov, Maramureş, Prahova, Satu Mare and Suceava. This is the largest category of county councils that are neither among the winners of PNDL nor among the winners of the previous programming period of EU funding. Nonetheless, they succeeded to absorb funds from the current programming period.
- Past and present EU winners, without being amongst PNDL winners. This is a set of past and present EU funds winners. Yet, these counties are not among the champions of State Budget funding. These are the counties of Călăraşi, Mehedinţi, Sălaj, Tulcea.

- 'Mix and match'—Present mixed funding approach. There are only two councils that presently combine top level of State Budget funding through PNDL and also succeeded to have an early start in European funding. These are the county councils of Arad and Gorj.
- All times winners (EU current and past and PNDL winners). Overall, from the entire set of 41 Romanian county councils analysed, only three of them are champions for all three funding lines. These are the counties of Bistriţa-Năsăud, Giurgiu and Vâlcea.

Furthermore, a part of the county councils from the category of State Budget winners is also in the top of largest shares of funding directed towards the county councils as compared to the sum allocated for the entire county from the same funding source, PNDL II. This means that for the counties of Neamţ, Ialomiţa and Vrancea, the level of funding allocated only to the County Council exceeds 30% of the total sum allocated for all the institutions within the corresponding county. It also means that the rest of the localities in the county have decreased financial opportunities for which to request funding, based on the fact that each county has, according to Fig. 5.4, a certain threshold of funding. This would further mean that, in cases of municipalities placed in these counties, results of PNDL II allocations are in particular competitive in relation to the County Council. Besides this, the counties of Teleorman and Vaslui are among the top performers regarding total sums allocated from PNDL per each county.[12]

Nevertheless, this typology reflects only a picture for the moment this analysis has been conducted. This picture can be changed, especially as the European funds absorption process will advance in the current programming period. In addition, there has also been another phase of funds' allocation through PNDL 2017–2020. An update of results' allocation for the year 2020 is presented in the sixth section of the book.

5.2.3 An Explanatory Model of the Absorption Results of PNDL for County Councils

A multiple regression model shows that the volume of PNDL funds at county level depends on the volume of EU funds absorbed in the previous period. Nevertheless, the sign of the relationship is indirect. In this respect, all other things being equal or held constant, a county council is more likely to have more funds from PNDL II as it has less population density and less developed absorption capacity of EU funds in the previous programming period, meaning it is not in the upper quartile of EU funds absorption (Fig. 5.5). The dependent variable is measured as the euro/inhabitant absorbed through PNDL II only by the county council from the respective county.[13]

[12]Top 5 on this indicator includes the counties of Suceava, Vaslui, Caraş Severin, Teleorman and Mehedinti.

[13]The regression model includes a logarithmic value of the total volume of funds.

Fig. 5.4 Typology of county councils

Therefore, in this model run for all the county councils receiving funds through PNDL II, predictors like the level of road infrastructure development (share of modernised county roads in the total length of county roads), political affiliation of County Council's Presidents, financial autonomy (share of own revenues in total revenues), receiving EU funds in the current programming period or size of the budget (level of expenditures for 2017) did not prove to act as significant predictors for the volume of funds per capita absorbed by each county council from PNDL II,

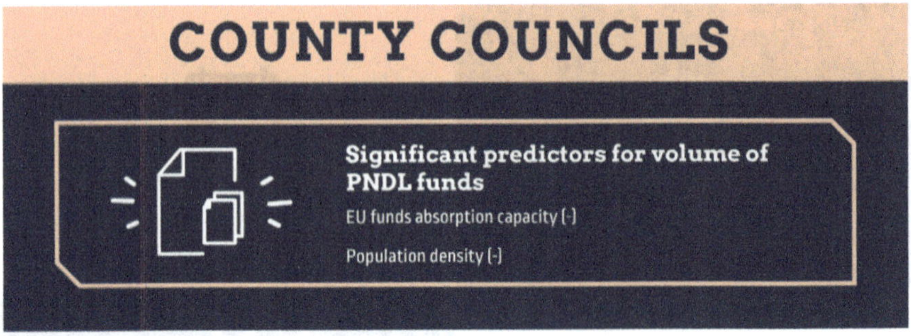

Fig. 5.5 Significant predictors for the volume of PNDL funds absorbed by County Councils (euro/inhabitant)

up to May 2018 (Table 5.5). In addition, alternative regression models,[14] including geographical demarcation (like localisation in South Muntenia development region) and level of human development, show similar results in terms of identification of significant predictors.

Furthermore, the qualitative research revealed the following aspects:

1. according to the interviewed stakeholders from the county level, the role of the County Council only included information meetings. Yet, the number of interviews is low, and it did not include political leaders, like the president of the County Council.

> there are no coordination meetings with the mayors, only information meetings, afterwards every locality applies for the projects they consider they need. I suppose that when they apply, they also take into account the investments conducted/ planned at the county level. In this programming period, the mayoralties from the rural area were not eligible to apply on the Regional Operational Program, whereas on the Rural National Development Program (PNDR) we really don't know at county level who applied on PNDR. Maybe those from the Prefecture conducted this centralisation with who applied on which funding line, we don't know this information at the level of County Council. (County Council representative, North-West development region)

2. Resource availability is considered from all lines of funding. Representatives of the County Councils declared that any funding opportunity is important, although PNDL II program has clearly different and simpler rules than European funding available. In addition, qualitative insights also revealed cases when the 'choice' of funding environment is limited, in the sense that by planning the process, the same principal as the one acting for PNDL II, namely MDRAP, can fix a narrow set of eligible beneficiaries. In this respect, the counties from the border have some 'mandatory projects' in the sense that they need to ensure the road infrastructure to the border, which applies to specific European-funded projects. These are funded through the territorial cooperation programs. In these cases,

[14]Including lower explanatory power.

Table 5.5 Main determinants for the volume of funds absorbed through PNDL 2017–2020 by the County Councils

	Unstandardised coefficients		Standardised coefficients			Collinearity statistics	
Predictors	B	Standard error	Beta	t	Sig.	Tolerance	VIF
(Constant)	6.256	0.733		8.537	0.000		
Share of own revenues in total revenues (2017) (%)	−0.018	0.016	−0.188	−1.127	0.268	0.676	1.479
Winners of EU funding 2009–2017	−0.697	0.275	−0.403	−2.533	0.017	0.740	1.352
Political affiliation of county council's president	0.090	0.247	0.055	0.364	0.718	0.822	1.216
Population Density	−0.153	0.054	−0.446	−2.861	0.007	0.771	1.297
Early starters of EU funding 2014–2020	0.160	0.224	0.103	0.717	0.479	0.902	1.109
Share of modernised county roads in the total length of county roads (%)	0.008	0.005	0.211	1.437	0.161	0.864	1.157
Size of the budget (2017)	−2.505E−9	0.000	−0.307	−1.856	0.073	0.686	1.457
Dependent variable: logarithmic volume of euro/inhabitant funds absorbed through PNDL 2017–2020 by each county council							

Data: Author's calculations based on an aggregated database with predictors explained in the Annex. (N=39). Linear regression method, Enter method, Adj. R2=0.28, Durbin-Watson test of 2.005. Note: Coloured cells indicate significant predictors for $p<0.05$

the policy scope for these County Councils is considerably influenced by vertical influence.

> we are not interested where the money comes from, we take from wherever we can, including PNDL II, Regional Operational Program and because we are a border county, we also take money from the cross-border programs, we take whatever we can. (County Council representative, North-West development region).

> we apply wherever we can to apply, but we are also a border county, and we have the responsibility to ensure the infrastructure for connecting the border. (County Council representative, West development region)

> I haven't worked at all on European funded projects, but I think they are complementary; values of the European-funded projects are much higher than in PNDL II, but it is still good that in PNDL II you can submit projects with a much lower value. (County Council representative, West development region)

3. problems related to insufficiently specialised personnel when compared to the number of approved projects have also been signalled.

> we help them with what we can, yet if we look at the number of projects we have, we also lack specialised personnel. (County Council representative, West development region)

4. problems related to transparency of projects and exclusion or inclusion criteria in the final list of contracts funded from PNDL II.

5. several recommendations have been issued in relation to PNDL II. Some of them regard increased transparency of the program, a better tailor-made approach for small communities that are not eligible for funding from other opportunities, a database with projects which can be searched in relation to various topics, etc. These recommendations are detailed in the last section of the book.

> I would say that for PNDL II transparency has been ensured only for some projects, for others not; I am talking now only of what I know, of the projects submitted by our County Council. (County Council representative, West development region)

5.3 Results at the Level of Municipalities

5.3.1 Results at the Level of Urban Municipalities

There are 944 projects awarded to urban municipalities within PNDL 2014–2020. Most of them are targeting educational institutions at different levels (470 projects) and transportation infrastructure—streets/parking places/bridges (300 projects). The rest of them aim the development of urban infrastructure regarding water and sewerage (116 projects), public lighting (7 projects), hospitals/ dispensaries (39 projects), mayoralties' offices[15] (7 projects) or other[16] type of projects (5 projects).

Yet, the rank of funds allocated by investment objectives is different from the number of contracted projects by the same criterion. For urban municipalities, most of the funds are targeting development of roads and bridges infrastructure, followed by educational infrastructure and water and sewerage. In addition, the mean value for this investment objective is higher for urban compared to rural municipalities.[17]

[15]Or rehabilitation of other public institutions' offices.

[16]Including complex projects targeting roads infrastructure, water and sewerage or projects with a too general label in order to be included in a specific category.

[17]The number of individual contracted projects for transportation infrastructure is much higher in the rural area compared to the urban area (1797 compared to 300 projects).

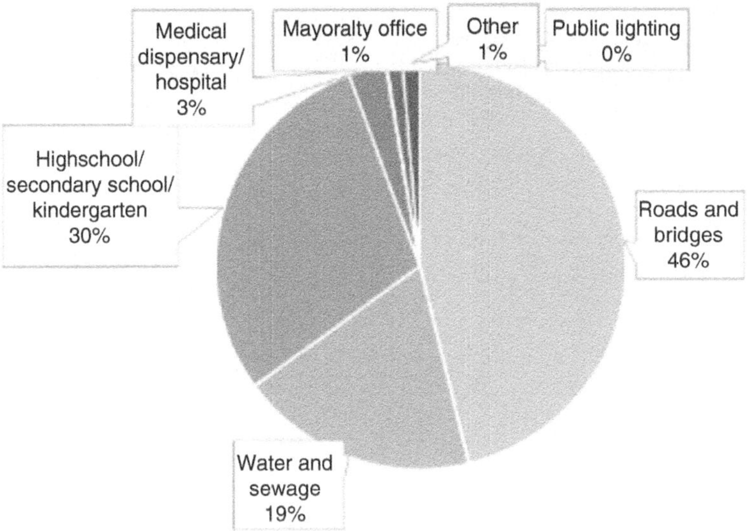

Fig. 5.6 PNDL II allocations by investment objectives for urban municipalities. Data: Author's calculations based on the information in the database of contracts awarded under PNDL 2017–2020

In a comparative view presented in the image above, for the rural area, the ranking of funds by investment objectives follows the same pattern as in the urban area (Figs. 5.6 and 5.7). Figures 5.6 and 5.7, there is a substantially larger share of funds contracted for the development of water and sewerage infrastructure in the rural area (39% of the total volume of funds compared to 19% in the urban area) and a lower level of investments in the educational infrastructure in the rural area (12% compared to 30% in the urban area).

Almost all urban municipalities (91%) received budgetary allocations from PNDL II, except for 30 localities (Table 5.6). Yet, it is worth mentioning that among those who received funds, some (8 municipalities) received small amounts from the contracted projects. An extended qualitative research might shed more light on this category of municipalities. For the case of rural municipalities, reasons for not having approved contracts included—not applying (as the municipality has already contracted funds from previous sessions of PNDL—PNDL I), problems of cadastre registration, lack of specialised personnel or 'we simply don't know why our project was rejected'. The next section details these reasons.

Within the total number of municipalities receiving funds through PNDL II, there is a small number of urban mayoralties contracting a large number of individual projects. The largest number of individual contracted projects belongs to the municipality of Târgovişte, Dâmboviţa county. Almost all projects of Târgovişte municipality are dedicated to the social infrastructure. More precisely, the approved projects are targeting medical offices in schools, kindergartens or high schools, including endowment of dentistry offices in schools or upgrading the building

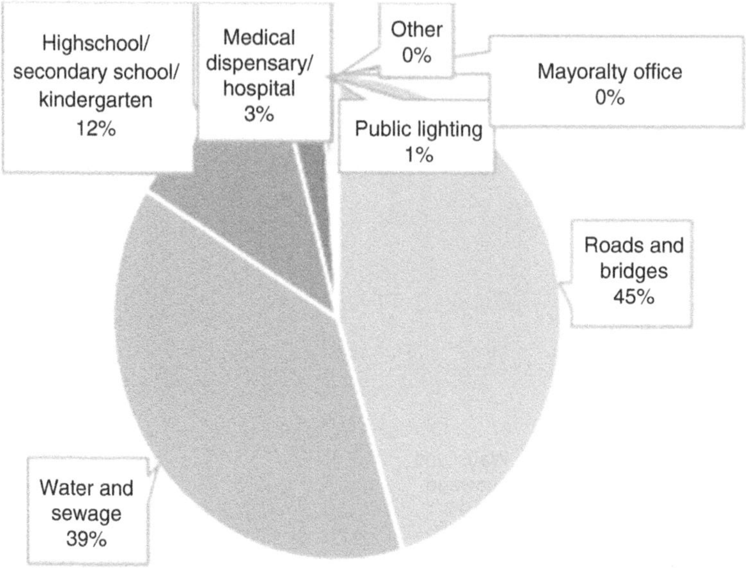

Fig. 5.7 PNDL II allocations by investment objectives for rural municipalities. Data: Author's calculations based on the information in the database of contracts awarded under PNDL 2017–2020

and equipment of nursery schools. Only one project of Târgovişte municipality envisages road infrastructure. In total, there are 40 projects contracted by this county residence municipality.

In the second and third place regarding the number of contracted projects are placed other county seat municipalities (Fig. 5.8). These are represented by the municipalities of Botoşani (Botoşani county) and Drobeta Turnu Severin (Mehedinţi county). Botoşani municipality has 35 projects, while Drobeta Turnu Severin has 14 contracts. Similar to the case of Târgovişte, both Botoşani and Drobeta Turnu Severin municipalities have focused investments on the educational units, namely firefighting authorisation for kindergartens, schools and high schools in the case of Botoşani, or upgrading of various types of educational units. Just as a reminder, the first priority set in PNDL II (according to the response to the public information request presented in the Annex) is represented by projects focusing on nursery schools and kindergartens, as well as schools without sanitary or emergency authorisation. On the contrary, there are also 93 municipalities with only one approved project from PNDL II. It is not clear whether, for instance, the municipality of Târgovişte has submitted 40 projects, and all these have been approved, or if the municipality of Zlatna (Alba county) has submitted 40 projects, and only one has been approved. This is because the number and type of projects submitted by applicants to PNDL have not been considered public information by the responsible Ministry (see the detailed response in the Annex).

Table 5.6 List of urban municipalities with zero funds from PNDL II

	Municipality	County
1.	CURTICI	ARAD
2.	COSTESTI	ARGES
3.	SLANIC MOLDOVA	BACAU
4.	ORADEA	BIHOR
5.	BEIUS	BIHOR
6.	VALEA LUI MIHAI	BIHOR
7.	BRASOV	BRASOV
8.	RASNOV	BRASOV
9.	FAUREI	BRAILA
10.	CARANSEBES	CARAŞ-SEVERIN
11.	MOLDOVA NOUĂ	CARAŞ-SEVERIN
12.	BAILESTI	DOLJ
13.	DABULENI	DOLJ
14.	BERESTI	GALATI
15.	BORSEC	HARGHITA
16.	VISEU DE SUS	MARAMURES
17.	DRAGANESTI-OLT	OLT
18.	PLOIESTI	PRAHOVA
19.	BREAZA	PRAHOVA
20.	PLOPENI	PRAHOVA
21.	SLANIC	PRAHOVA
22.	URLATI	PRAHOVA
23.	CISNADIE	SIBIU
24.	SUCEAVA	SUCEAVA
25.	LUGOJ	TIMIS
26.	SINICOLAUL MARE	TIMIS
27.	RECAS	TIMIS
28.	VASLUI	VASLUI
29.	PANCIU	VRANCEA
30.	POPESTI LEORDENI	ILFOV

Data: Author's calculations based on the information in the database of contracts awarded under PNDL 2017–2020

Nonetheless, the municipalities with the highest number of contracted projects do not represent the applicants from the urban area with the largest volume of approved funds. Tables below present data computed in total volume, transformed in euro (Table 5.7), or reported to the population size (euro/inhabitant) (Table 5.8). Taken into consideration the indicator on euro/inhabitant, these are represented by the urban municipalities of Mioveni (Argeş county), Satu Mare (Satu Mare county) or Bistriţa (Bistriţa–Năsăud county). In a similar manner, the highest volume of funds (euro) has been contracted by the municipalities of Predeal, Vînju Mare and Măcin. Just as an example, the municipality of Predeal has only two

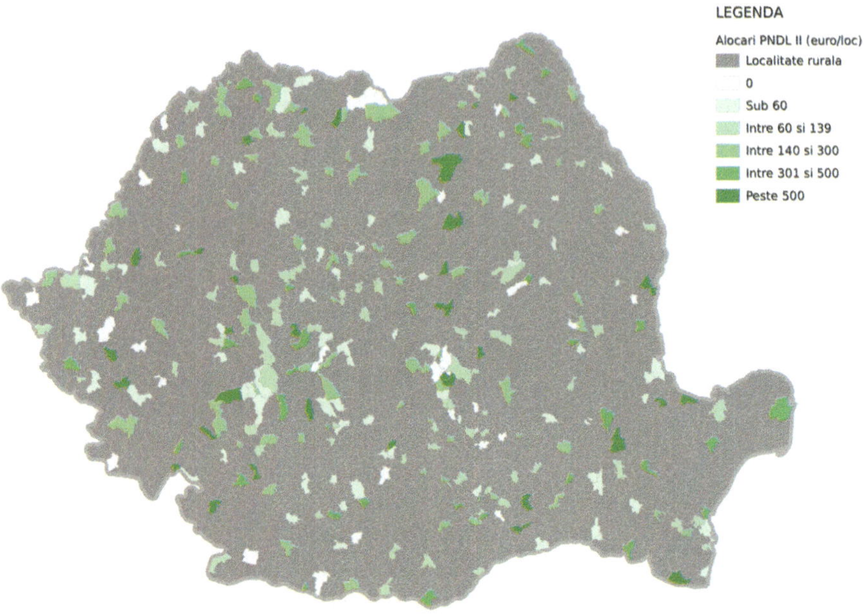

Fig. 5.8 Distribution of PNDL funds at the level of urban municipalities. Data: Author's calculations based on the information in the database of contracts awarded under PNDL 2017–2020. Note: the map presents the distribution of funds for urban municipalities (as euro/inhabitant)

projects approved—one on upgrading and rehabilitation of a school, and the other one on road infrastructure, upgrading streets.[18] Nevertheless, their sum makes a considerable amount, higher than that of the 40 projects approved for Târgovişte municipality. Moreover, reporting the total volume of funds to the population, in the case of Predeal, might not yield an accurate picture of the needs in terms of infrastructure development.[19] Furthermore, the municipality of Mioveni has also contracted projects regarding only the social infrastructure—two on educational infrastructure and one on health infrastructure—construction of a town hospital. This last project will also be discussed in relation to the new context of COVID-19 pandemic, in the section on the relevance of studying PNDL in the context of the COVID-19 global crisis. In Satu Mare on the other hand, two projects, one on road infrastructure and the other one on water and sewerage, place this municipality in the second place among the urban municipalities with the largest volume of funds per capita.

A special position in these two rankings is held by the municipality of Măcin (Tulcea county). It has top positions (in the first ten places) on both types of

[18] Title of the project: Upgrading streets in the town of Predeal—second phase.

[19] It is possible that the building land area might have been changed in the case of Predeal.

Table 5.7 Top 10 urban municipalities with maximum allocations from PNDL II (euro/inhabitants)

	Municipality	County
1.	PREDEAL	BRASOV
2.	VINJU MARE	MEHEDINTI
3.	MACIN	TULCEA
4.	NEGRU VODĂ	CONSTANŢA
5.	MIERCUREA SIBIULUI	SIBIU
6.	PRIMARIA DRAGOMIRESTI	MARAMURES
7.	BUDESTI	CALARASI
8.	MUNICIPIU ORSOVA	MEHEDINTI
9.	MURGENI	VASLUI
10.	SIMERIA	HUNEDOARA

Data: Author's calculations based on the information in the database of contracts awarded under PNDL 2017–2020

Table 5.8 Top 10 urban municipalities with maximum allocations from PNDL II (euro)

	Municipality	County
1.	MIOVENI	ARGES
2.	SATU MARE	SATU MARE
3.	BISTRITA	BISTRITA-NASAUD
4.	NĂVODARI	CONSTANŢA
5.	GHEORGHENI	HARGHITA
6.	BOCŞA	CARAŞ-SEVERIN
7.	MACIN	TULCEA
8.	SIMERIA	HUNEDOARA
9.	MIERCUREA-CIUC	HARGHITA
10.	VOLUNTARI	ILFOV

Data: Author's calculations based on the information in the database of contracts awarded under PNDL 2017–2020

ranking—total volume or volume of funds per capita. The municipality has contracted four projects under PNDL II. Amongst these, three of them are dedicated to schools—rehabilitation, upgrading and endowment of school infrastructure, namely two secondary schools and one high school. The fourth project from Măcin focuses on upgrading the road infrastructure. A similar position, present in both types of ranking, is for the municipality of Simeria (Hunedoara county), with five contracted projects. The municipality succeeded in securing projects on both the educational infrastructure (one secondary school and one high school), as well as on the water network (one project) and road infrastructure (two projects).

Furthermore, on the types of supported investments, there are some examples worth mentioning. One is for the municipality of Târgu Jiu (Gorj county) which has been awarded a contract for upgrading and rehabilitation of a protected area of the monument area Calea Eroilor. It is difficult to include in an investment priority this project. Furthermore, a similar type of project has been rejected in the case of Satu

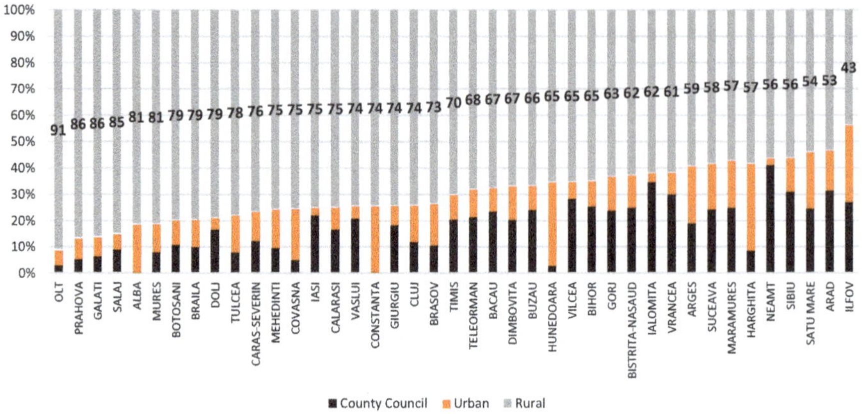

Fig. 5.9 PNDL allocations—shares by county councils, urban and rural municipalities
Data: Author's calculations based on the information in the database of contracts awarded under PNDL 2017–2020. Note. For the county of Harghita, the sum of shares equals 97.38%, as the allocations from PNDL 2 also include projects awarded to intercommunity development associations.

Mare County Museum (Satu Mare County Council—see previously presented list of projects submitted in the county of Satu Mare, Table 3.4). Again, a transparent publishing of selection results, including all the submitted proposals as well as reasons for rejection/ approval would most likely make it clear why similar projects result in different status concerning funding for PNDL II.

The largest shares of volume of funds awarded to rural municipalities are for the counties of Olt, Prahova, Galati, Sălaj, Alba and Mureş (above 80% of the total volume of funds for each county) Fig. 5.9. In all these counties, the county councils have very small amounts of shares from the total sum.

An analysis of PNDL allocations shows that the category of urban municipalities with high absorption rate (more than 500 euro/inhabitant) is predominantly based on small urban municipalities, with low scores for human development index (lower and lower medium quartiles), in the lower quartiles of population density (lower and lower medium quartiles), which are part of a Local Action Group,[20] with a poor road infrastructure (low share of modernised roads within the total length of municipal roads) and in the lower quartile of the organisation size (Table 5.9). Therefore, according to these findings, it seems that it has been an accurate targeting of funds for urban municipalities. Yet, the mayor's political affiliation plays a role in those municipalities with zero funds. In a significantly larger share, these municipalities have a mayor with a different political affiliation than the ruling one. Nevertheless, it is difficult to state whether they applied to these funds and did not succeed or never applied for attracting these financial resources to the local budget. This topic

[20] See the Annex for variables' operationalisation. According to European funding rules, only urban municipalities with less than 20,000 inhabitants can be part of a Local Action Group.

Table 5.9 Data on PNDL allocations for urban municipalities

Indicators		PNDL allocations for Romanian urban[a] municipalities					
Development region		Zero funds	Low	Lower medium	Higher medium	High	Total
	Bucharest-Ilfov	*	*	*	*	0	100
	Centre	*	17.5	24.6	38.6	12.3	100
	North West	*	18.6	*	58.1	*	100
	West	14.3	21.4	*	45.2	11.9	100
	South West	*	22.5	15.0	42.5	12.5	100
	South Muntenia	12.5	20.8	14.6	43.8	*	100
	South East	*	17.1	*	57.1	*	100
	North East	*	21.7	19.6	41.3	*	100
	Total (%)	9.4	19.7	14.1	46.1	10.7	100
	N	30	63	45	147	34	319
European funds absorption 2009–2017	Zero funds	13.2	*	*	57.9	15.8	100
	Low absorption	6.9	18.8	13.9	48.5	11.9	100
	Medium absorption	10.6	25.8	17.4	37.9	8.3	100
	High absorption	*	18.8	*	54.2	10.4	100
	Total (%)	9.4	19.7	14.1	46.1	10.7	100
	N	30	63	45	147	34	319
Human development index	Lower quartile	10.1	*	8.9	55.7	20.3	100
	Low medium quartile	10.1	12.7	7.6	51.9	17.7	100
	High medium quartile	*	17.5	21.3	56.3	*	100
	High	13.9	44.3	19.0	19.0	*	100
	Total (%)	9.5	19.9	14.2	45.7	10.7	100
	N	30	63	45	145	34	317
Mayor's political affiliation	Different from the ruling party	12.9	21.3	13.5	42.6	9.7	100
	Ruling party (PSD)	6.1	18.3	14.6	49.4	11.6	100
	Total (%)	9.4	19.7	14.1	46.1	10.7	100
	N	30	63	45	147	34	319

(continued)

Table 5.9 (continued)

Indicators		PNDL allocations for Romanian urban municipalities					
CC president's political affiliation	Different from the ruling party	8.5	17.8	16.9	44.9	11.9	100
	Ruling party (PSD)	10.0	20.9	12.4	46.8	10.0	100
	Total (%)	9.4	19.7	14.1	46.1	10.7	100
	N	30	63	45	147	34	319
Population density	Lower quartile	7.5	6.3	10.0	58.8	17.5	100
	Low medium quartile	10.0	11.3	8.8	52.5	17.5	100
	High medium quartile	10.0	18.8	20.0	43.8	7.5	100
	High	10.1	43.0	17.7	29.1	0.0	100
	Total (%)	9.4	19.7	14.1	46.1	10.7	100
	N	30	63	45	147	34	319
Early starters of new EF	Without European funds	9.7	18.1	13.4	45.8	13.0	100
	With European funds	8.7	23.3	15.5	46.6	5.8	100
	Total (%)	9.4	19.7	14.1	46.1	10.7	100
	N	30	63	45	147	34	319
Part of a local action Group (LAG)	Not part of a LAG	8.8	28.0	15.5	39.9	7.8	100.0
	Part of a LAG	10.3	7.1	11.9	55.6	15.1	100.0
	Total (%)	9.4	19.7	14.1	46.1	10.7	100
	N	30	63	45	147	34	319
Length of modernised roads	Lower quartile	9.5	7.1	8.3	54.8	20.2	100
	Low medium quartile	8.8	*	13.8	60.0	13.8	100
	High medium quartile	6.6	25.0	17.1	44.7	6.6	100
	High	12.7	44.3	17.7	24.1	*	100
	Total (%)	9.4	19.7	14.1	46.1	10.7	100
	N	30	63	45	147	34	319
Categories of organisation size	Lower quartile	7.4	7.4	9.9	50.6	24.7	100
	Low medium quartile	7.5	6.3	7.5	67.5	11.3	100
	High medium quartile	13.6	13.6	18.5	48.1	6.2	100
	High	9.1	53.2	20.8	16.9	0.0	100
	Total (%)	9.4	19.7	14.1	46.1	10.7	100
	N	30	63	45	147	34	319

Data: Author's calculations based on the information in the database of contracts awarded under PNDL 2017-2020. Coloured cells indicate values significantly higher. Note: * Under 5 cases

[a] For the urban municipalities the categories established for the volume of funds (euro/inhabitant) are as follows: Zero funds, Low absorption (less or equal to 50 euro/inhabitant), Lower medium (Higher than 50 and less or equal to 100 euro/ inhabitant), Higher medium (Higher or equal to 101 and less or equal to 500 euro/inhabitant) and High (higher than 500 euro/inhabitant)

Fig. 5.10 Significant predictors for volume of funds absorbed through PNDL by urban municipalities (euro/inhabitant)

is related to the lack of transparency of the application procedure, which stands out in the Ministry of Regional Development and Public Administration's official response to the public information request (see the section on Annexes for the detailed response).

A multiple regression model shows that, all other things being equal or held constant, an urban municipality is more likely to have more funds from PNDL as it is less developed according to the human development index, it has fewer positions in the organisational size (based on the maximum number of available positions as stated in the law), is located in a county with an experienced President of the County Council (more than 10 years in the position of County Council President), and it is within a county with less administrative units (Fig. 5.10 and Table 5.10).

From these findings, it follows that a resource outside of the organisation itself has proved to play a role in accessing a higher volume of funds from PNDL II, in the case of urban municipalities from Romania. It is represented by the length of tenure of the President of the County Council. Yet, this role most likely is differentiated according to the level and type of dependence each municipality has. In our model, municipalities less developed tend to have a higher volume of funds per inhabitant. Furthermore, another variable outside of the organisation plays a role, namely the number of administrative units in the county. This variable signals the number of competitors within the organisational field of largest State Budget funded programs. Just as a reminder, according to the official response received from MDRAP, prioritisation criteria for PNDL II include, among others, the weight of the number of administrative-territorial units in the county as a share of the total number of administrative-territorial units at the national level. Moreover, specific investment objective lines mention that, initially, one project for each territorial administrative unit is awarded.

In addition, it should be noted that the volume of funds does not depend on the infrastructure status, be it related to the length of modernised roads (or share of modernised roads in the total length of urban roads) or to the length of water networks. These independent variables are not introduced in the presented

Table 5.10 Main determinants of PNDL allocations for urban municipalities

	Unstandardised coefficients		Standardised coefficients			Collinearity statistics	
Predictors	B	Standard error	Beta	t	Sig.	Tolerance	VIF
Constant	7.664	0.484		15.828	0.000		
Human development index	−0.027	0.006	−0.304	−4.736	0.000	0.565	1.770
Mayor is from the ruling party (PSD)	0.131	0.104	0.062	1.255	0.211	0.955	1.047
CC president's political affiliation	0.184	0.131	0.076	1.405	0.161	0.806	1.241
CC president's experience (more than 10 years)	0.307	0.133	0.122	2.305	0.022	0.823	1.214
Organisational size	−0.002	0.000	−0.361	−5.705	0.000	0.582	1.719
EU funds absorption capacity	1.202E−5	0.000	0.003	0.065	0.948	0.932	1.073
No of administrative units per county	−0.009	0.003	−0.153	−3.023	0.003	0.908	1.101

Dependent variable: logarithmic volume of funds absorbed through PNDL 2017–2020 by each urban municipality (euro/inhabitant)

Data: Author's calculations based on an aggregated database with predictors explained in the Annex. (N=277). Linear regression method, Enter method, Adj. R2=0.358, Durbin-Watson test of 2.19. Note: Coloured cells indicate significant predictors for $p<0.05$

model due to correlation problems—large municipalities also have large sizes of population and large lengths of modernised roads and water networks. However, different alternative regression models have been tested for this type of territorial administrative units, similar to the work conducted at county and urban municipalities' level. The analysis also considered population size, and it proved to be a significant predictor in the same direction as organisational size.

5.3.2 *Results at the Level of Rural Municipalities*

General Results

Data analysis at a national level shows that there are 80 localities in rural Romania which are white spots on both key dimensions of extra budgetary funding, both national and European. Yet, this analysis has not taken into consideration all types of national funding, like previous funding sessions from PNDL or other State Budged funded programs. This category only points out that this set of 80 municipalities received zero funding from both PNDL II as well as all types of European funds available in the period of 2009–2017. Out of these, 19 localities have a poor level of technical and building equipment (transportation, water, gas infrastructure, density of public roads network). They deserve special attention in what concerns local development policies. Their development needs should be included in programming documents at both local, county and national level. The qualitative research conducted for this study revealed problems with asymmetric information at agents' level (project proposals submitted to the County Councils instead of the Ministry), cadastre registration, lack of specialised personnel, etc. On this point, the sixth section of the book (Update 2020: Has anything changed in between) offers a detailed update for 2020, including this set of rural municipalities that did not succeed in secluding funds from PNDL II (Table 5.11).

The following tables present the top 10 rural municipalities with maximum allocations from PNDL II, both as total volumes of funds as well as funds reported to the size of population (Tables 5.12 and 5.13). Tables 5.12 and 5.13, the top 3 on both types of ranking are held by communes from two counties: Caraş-Severin

Table 5.11 List of rural municipalities with a low level of infrastructure development and zero funding from both PNDL and European funds

	Municipality	County
1.	PETRIS	ARAD
2.	LAZURI DE BEIUS	BIHOR
3.	DIMACHENI	BOTOSANI
4.	ODAILE	BUZAU
5.	OCNA DE FIER	Caraş-SEVERIN
6.	BOTOSESTI-PAIA	DOLJ
7.	DOBROTESTI	DOLJ
8.	DOBRESTI	DOLJ
9.	SILISTEA CRUCII	DOLJ
10.	COSOVENI	DOLJ
11.	LIPOVU	DOLJ
12.	SLIVILESTI	GORJ
13.	BARBULESTI	IALOMITA
14.	MILCOV	OLT
15.	SALCIA	PRAHOVA
16.	CIUPERCENI	TELEORMAN
17.	RASMIRESTI	TELEORMAN
18.	BARA	TIMIS
19.	I.C.BRATIANU	TULCEA

Data: Author's calculations based on the information in the database of contracts awarded under PNDL 2017–2020 and local budgets' execution

Table 5.12 Top 10 rural municipalities with maximum allocations from PNDL II (euro)

	Municipality	County
1.	CORNEREVA	CARAŞ-SEVERIN
2.	BAUTAR	CARAŞ-SEVERIN
3.	RIU DE MORI	HUNEDOARA
4.	CERNA	TULCEA
5.	MUNTENI BUZAU	IALOMITA
6.	TURNU RUIENI	CARAŞ-SEVERIN
7.	PLOPIS	SALAJ
8.	MARCA	SALAJ
9.	SARICHIOI	TULCEA
10.	LUNCAVITA	TULCEA

Data: Author's calculations based on the information in the database of contracts awarded under PNDL 2017–2020

Table 5.13 Top 10 rural municipalities with maximum allocations from PNDL II (euro/inhabitants)

	Municipality	County
1.	BREBU NOU	CARAŞ-SEVERIN
2.	BUNILA	HUNEDOARA
3.	BULZESTI	HUNEDOARA
4.	CERU BACAINTI	ALBA
5.	VULTURU	CONSTANŢA
6.	RIMET	ALBA
7.	MICESTII DE CIMPIE	BISTRITA-NASAUD
8.	LUDOS	SIBIU
9.	BAUTAR	CARAŞ-SEVERIN
10.	BICHIS	MURES

Data: Author's calculations based on the information in the database of contracts awarded under PNDL 2017–2020

and Hunedoara. Some of them are also among the champions of EU funds; such is the case of Luncaviţa, Tulcea county. For the case of PNDL II, Luncaviţa has four approved projects, two on road infrastructure, one on sewerage and one on public lighting. Yet, the 'champions' among communes in terms of total volume of funds absorbed are represented by two communes in Caraş-Severin (Cornereva and Băuţari) and one placed in Hunedoara (Rîu de Mori). Amongst them, Băuţari holds a special position as it is also present in the top 10 rural maximum allocations from PNDL II, if reporting the total volume of funds absorbed to the population. There are four projects approved for this commune, all of them on top 3 priorities mentioned in the prioritisation criteria as stated by MDRAP in response to the public information request: school infrastructure (rehabilitation and upgrading of secondary school), roads (two projects) and sewerage and wastewater treatment station (one project). In a similar manner, Cornereva has five projects focusing on the same top 3 priorities, yet also including health infrastructure—dispensary as well as water supply network. Nevertheless, these are not the only projects Cornereva has. A list of successful projects (with signed funding contracts) published by the Prefecture of Caraş-Severin[21] lists two previously funded projects from PNDL (signed in 2015) and two other projects on the same funding priorities as PNDL—communal roads and educational infrastructure (contracts signed in 2017). These last two projects have been funded from the National Rural Development Program, submeasure 7.2.—*Investments in creating and upgrading of basic infrastructure at a small scale*. They fund upgrading of communal roads and, respectively, rehabilitation, upgrading, extending and endowment of agriculture vocational school in Bogiltin, Cornereva commune. The two project titles about the communal roads with two different sources of funding (PNDL II and National Rural Development Program) do not offer sufficient information for an accurate distinction between distinct yet similar investment objectives. This is why, as already stated, there is a pressing need to coordinate the investment objectives at a central level and, at the same, also publish transparent and complete information about the outcomes of funding sessions.

Furthermore, in the second type of ranking, there are communes with very low population size; hence, the total volume of funds reported to population results in high values. In this respect, the commune of Brebu Nou, with important touristic potential, has three successful projects on PNDL II: two on road network and one on water supply network. Brebu Nou had one other project previously funded from PNDL (contract signed in 2015) for a new water supply system in the commune of Gărâna.[22] The second place commune has both projects focused on upgrading the communal road infrastructure.

An analysis of PNDL allocations shows that there are significant discrepancies between categories of rural municipalities established according to the volume of funds received through PNDL (Table 5.14), as follows:

- The category of rural municipalities receiving zero funds is in a significantly higher share from the development regions of Bucharest-Ilfov, Centre and West. Furthermore, they are from the type of municipalities with no European funds neither in the previous programming period nor in the current one. In addition, they represent a category of municipalities which score high according to the Human development Index and on infrastructure development index, and have their mayor and the President of the County Council (from the county they are located in) with a different political affiliation than the ruling party.
- In the category of rural municipalities with a lower medium volume of funds absorbed through PNDL (higher than 50 and less or equal to 200 euro/inhabitant), the municipalities from Bucharest-Ilfov and North-East development regions,

[21] Available at: https://cs.prefectura.mai.gov.ro/wp-content/uploads/sites/33/2018/08/ilovepdf_merged.pdf (date of access: September 6, 2020).

[22] According to the information published by Prefecture Institution, available at: https://cs.prefectura.mai.gov.ro/wp-content/uploads/sites/33/2018/08/ilovepdf_merged.pdf (date of access: September 6, 2020).

Table 5.14 Data on PNDL allocations for rural municipalities

Indicators		PNDL allocations for Romanian rural municipalities[a]					
Development region		funds Zero	Low	Lower medium	Higher medium	High	Total
	Bucharest-Ilfov	21.9	*	40.6	25	0	100
	Centre	15.4	1.7	15.1	36.7	31.1	100
	North West	11.4	5.2	17.1	41.2	25.1	100
	West	13.5	2.8	14.2	36.3	33.1	100
	South West	6.4	3.9	12.5	46.8	30.4	100
	South Muntenia	10.2	4.8	16.6	47.8	20.6	100
	South East	6.8	3.4	13.5	45.6	30.7	100
	North East	3	4.5	22.9	52.6	17	100
	Total (%)	9.2	4.0	16.7	44.5	25.6	100
	N	264	115	477	1274	731	2861
European funds 2009–2017	Not in the upper quartile	9.1	4.5	16.8	45.0	24.7	100
	In the upper quartile	6.6	2.7	16.9	44.7	29.1	100
	Total (%)	8.5	4.1	16.8	44.9	25.8	100
	N	241	115	477	1274	731	2838
Human development index	Lower quartile	6.6	2.2	12.4	42.5	36.4	100
	Low medium quartile	8.0	4.5	13.4	47.5	26.5	100
	High medium quartile	7.0	5.1	18.1	46.4	23.4	100
	High	13.6	4.8	23.6	45.4	12.6	100
	Total (%)	8.8	4.2	16.9	45.5	24.7	100
	N	241	114	463	1246	677	2741
Mayor's political affiliation	Different from the ruling party	12.7	4.6	17.6	40.9	24.2	100
	Ruling party (PSD)	6.5	3.6	16.0	47.4	26.6	100
	Total (%)	9.2	4.0	16.7	44.5	25.6	100
	N	264	115	477	1274	731	2861
CC president's political affiliation	Different from the ruling party	13.5	4.0	19.5	39.6	23.4	100
	Ruling party (PSD)	7.5	4.0	15.5	46.5	26.4	100
	Total (%)	9.2	4.0	16.7	44.5	25.6	100
	N	264	115	477	1274	731	2861

(continued)

Table 5.14 (continued)

Indicators		PNDL allocations for Romanian rural municipalities					
Population density	Low population density	7.6	3.4	14.7	40.2	34.1	100
	Medium population density	10.3	3.7	16.6	43.3	26.1	100
	High population density	9.5	5.0	18.6	50.0	16.9	100
	Total (%)	9.2	4.0	16.7	44.5	25.6	100
	N	264	115	477	1274	731	2861
Infrastructure development	Lower quartile	7.5	2.8	13.0	45.0	31.7	100
	Low medium quartile	7.0	3.6	15.6	44.9	29.0	100
	High medium quartile	8.7	5.7	16.8	44.4	24.5	100
	High	14.3	4.2	22.2	43.7	15.6	100
	Total (%)	9.2	4.0	16.7	44.5	25.6	100
	N	264	115	477	1274	731	2861
Early starters of new EF	Without European funds	10.3	3.4	15.3	44.1	26.8	100
	With European funds	6.9	5.3	19.5	45.5	22.9	100
	Total (%)	9.2	4.0	16.7	44.5	25.6	100
	N	264	115	477	1274	731	2861
Part of a local action group (LAG)	Not part of LAG	12.1	4.2	17.8	43.5	22.4	100
	Part of LAG	9.0	4.0	16.6	44.6	25.8	100
	Total (%)	9.2	4.0	16.7	44.5	25.6	100
	N	264	115	477	1274	731	2861

Data: Author's calculations based on the information in the database of contracts awarded under PNDL 2017–2020. Coloured cells indicate values significantly higher. Note: * Under 5 cases

[a] For the rural municipalities the categories established for the volume of funds (euro/inhabitant) are as follows: Zero funds, Low absorption (less or equal to 50 euro/inhabitant), Lower medium (Higher than 50 and less or equal to 200 euro/ inhabitant), Higher medium (Higher than 200 and less or equal to 800 euro/inhabitant) and High (higher than 800 euro/inhabitant)

with a high score on human development index, a high absorption rate of EU funds in the previous programming period accompanied by a good start in the current programming period (with European funds among early starters of the present EU funding cycle) and those from counties where the President of the County Council has a different political affiliation than the ruling party predominate.

- Mayor's political affiliation differentiates only among the categories of municipalities with zero funds (where predominate mayors with a different political affiliation than that of the ruling party) and in the category with a higher medium volume of funds (where mayors with the same political affiliation as the ruling party predominate). Similar differentiations can be found concerning the political affiliation of the president of the county council (within the same categories of municipalities and the same direction of association).

To refine the results presented above, a multiple regression analysis has been conducted and is presented below (Table 5.15).

A multiple regression model shows that, all other things being equal or held constant, a rural municipality is more likely to have more funds from PNDL II as it is less developed according to the human development index, its mayor has the same political affiliation as the ruling party, it is located within South-East or South-West development regions, it has a population size under 3000 inhabitants, it has less developed infrastructure development, a smaller organisational size, and it is placed within a county with less administrative units (Fig. 5.10 and Table 5.15). Alternative predictive models have been tested, yet their explanatory power is lower than the one of the presented model. In addition, problems of multicollinearity have also been detected in other models. To conclude, there is room for improving the predictive model, at least for the rural mayoralties. The difficulty of finding a better explanatory model most likely lies within the significant disparities between the rural mayoralties (Figs. 5.11 and 5.12). It can also be caused by other factors as signalled by the qualitative research—such as the level of absorbed funds from previous sessions of PNDL (PNDL I), problems with cadastre registration, or other issues further detailed by representatives of rural municipalities participating in the research.

Qualitative research showed, according to the opinions expressed by representatives of communes and small urban areas, specific issues related to:

1. asymmetric information between agents. In addition, a perceived asymmetric result dependency in relation to the County Council. It is important to state that it is about a case of a local authority representative from a commune with a low level of infrastructure development and zero funding from both PNDL and European funds. Thus, according to the information provided by the respondents, draft projects have been submitted to the county council, not directly to the Ministry, and mayors have been waiting for answers from county level, instead of the principal level. The Mayoralty representative perceives an asymmetric result dependency in relation to the County Council.

> I tried on PNDL II, I've prepared the file, there was a meeting there at the County Council, and we have been told to come up with as many projects as possible; but when I came with the project (on sewage systems) the president of the County Council gave me back the file and told me it's too late, and it's not possible anymore, maybe next time.

> After this, they also called us to come to the County Council, and they told us to do projects on the gas network, but after we have done the project, they told us that there is no funding source. (Mayoralty representative, South development region)

Table 5.15 Main determinants of PNDL allocations for rural municipalities

	Unstandardised coefficients		Standardised coefficients			Collinearity statistics	
Predictors	B	Standard error	Beta	t	Sig.	Tolerance	VIF
Constant	7.196	.175		41.110	0.000		
Human development index	−0.010	0.002	−0.106	−4.096	0.000	0.513	1.949
Mayor's political affiliation (PSD)	0.094	0.040	0.045	2.326	0.020	0.939	1.064
CC president's political affiliation	−0.018	0.056	−0.006	−0.313	0.754	0.856	1.168
Early starters of EU funding 2014–2020	−0.056	0.042	−0.025	−1.325	0.185	0.941	1.063
Infrastructure Development	−0.452	0.210	−0.052	−2.147	0.032	0.583	1.717
No of administrative units per county	−0.008	0.001	−0.154	−8.075	0.000	0.949	1.054
It is located in south east or south west	0.106	0.046	0.045	2.297	0.022	0.889	1.125
EU funds absorption 2009–2017 (euro/inhab)	1.889E−5	0.000	0.009	0.475	0.635	0.922	1.084
Part of a LAG	0.013	0.075	0.003	0.176	0.860	0.990	1.010
Population density	−0.007	0.005	−0.028	−1.429	0.153	0.898	1.113
Organisational size	−0.005	0.002	−0.064	−3.113	0.002	0.819	1.221
Above average fiscal capacity	0.077	0.048	0.033	1.591	0.112	0.783	1.277
Population size under 3000 inhab	0.439	0.044	0.211	9.871	0.000	0.757	1.321

Dependent variable: logarithmic volume of funds absorbed through PNDL 2017–2020 by each rural municipality (euro/inhabitant)

Data: author's calculations based on an aggregated database with predictors explained in the Annex. (N=2497). Linear regression method, Enter method, Adj. R2=0.14, Durbin-Watson test of 1.92. Note: Coloured cells indicate significant predictors for p<0.05

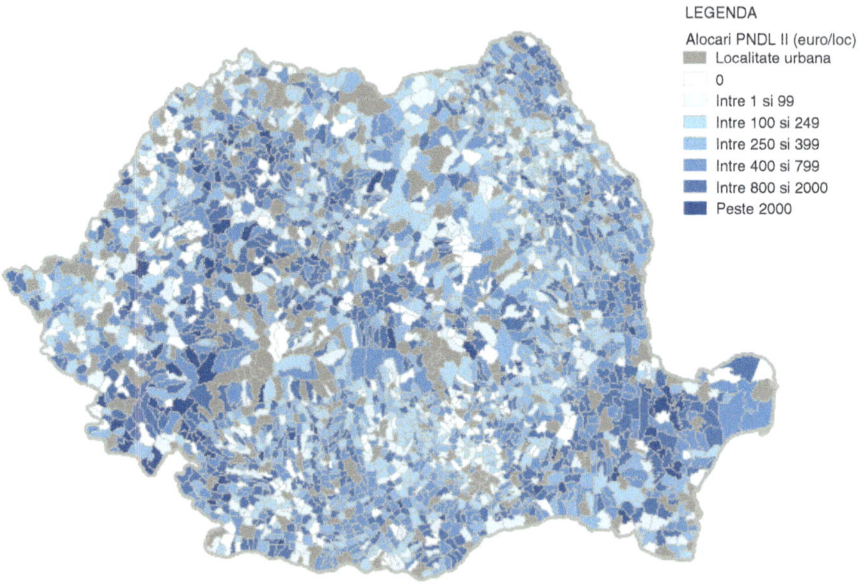

Fig. 5.11 Distribution of PNDL funds at the level of rural municipalities. Data: author's calculations based on the information in the database of contracts awarded under PNDL 2017–2020. Note: The map presents the distribution of funds for rural municipalities (as euro/inhabitant)

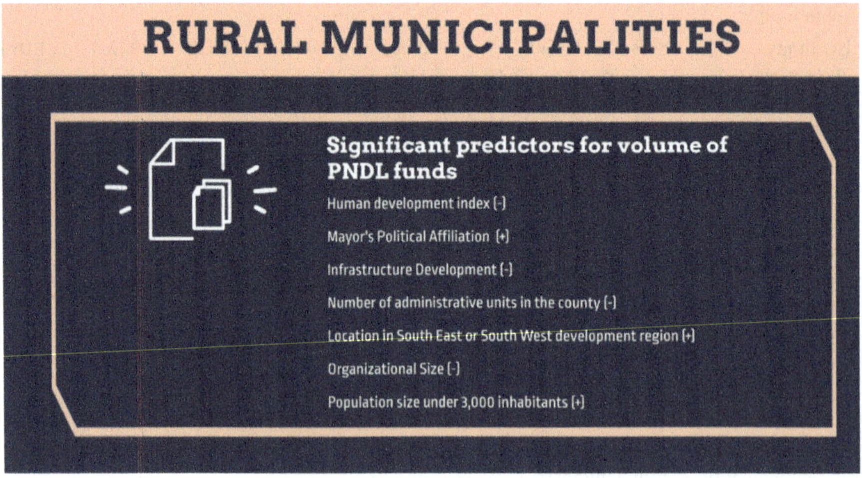

Fig. 5.12 Significant predictors for volume of funds absorbed through PNDL by rural municipalities (euro/inhabitant)

2. statements considering there have been cases of discrimination on the ethnical composition of localities and/or leadership representation. Leaders of Roma communities considered that their locality had been deprived of PNDL II funds as a result of their ethnical background.

> We definitely need investments in water and sewage. After a flood in 2015, the water is no longer potable. I have the project, I have it here in a rack if you want it, but you see our commune is a new one, it has been separated from a larger commune in 2005. At the present time, we are part of a Local Action Group, but we received nothing except for a backhoe from AFIR (Agency for Funding Rural Investments).[23] I need to tell you that I am a Roma ethnic, and you know how is the case with Roma people, I think that this plays a role, too. (Mayoralty representative, South development region)

3. cases of adaptive leadership in the form of a process variable, in which action preferences change based on previous experience with the first phase of program implementation or in relation to other factors. In this case, some leaders never applied to the second phase of PNDL, as they had successful projects in the first phase and considered the funds from the second phase should be allocated to other communes. Furthermore, rural community leaders declared that some municipalities, namely those with low population size, face a similar environmental context, which would most likely lead to an institutional isomorphism '*We, as small communes, under 1000 inhabitants, we have no other chance to pave the roads*'. This would mean, most likely, that, at least as perceived, the only available funding line is that of submitting projects to PNDL. Therefore, it is not surprising that these communes have sent further projects that have not been successful under PNDL II to similar funding lines, like FDI—Fund for Development and Initiatives. As their financial autonomy is rather low, it means a higher dependence on the support of vital resources in the form of a narrow set of funding lines. Consequently, this resembles more of a coercive type of institutional isomorphism, in line with DiMaggio and Powell's work (1983).

Yet, these findings are only based on perceptions of the funding environment. As already mentioned, organisations are influenced and able to influence their funding environment. At least for part of the rural areas, an additional funding line is represented by the EU funds from the National Rural Development Plan. Nevertheless, further conditions can also restrict their opportunities for securing funding from it.

> I thought it would be unfair compared to my colleagues from other communes to apply and maybe win again, I know cases of communes who have nothing, no funds at all.
>
> I don't have projects on PNDL II, but the neighbouring communes have, and I tell you there is another face of the commune, there is a step forward, there has been a success for poor communes. We, as small communes, under 1000 inhabitants, we have no other chance to pave the roads. (Mayoralty representative, South-East development region)

[23] Responsible for implementing the National Rural Development Program.

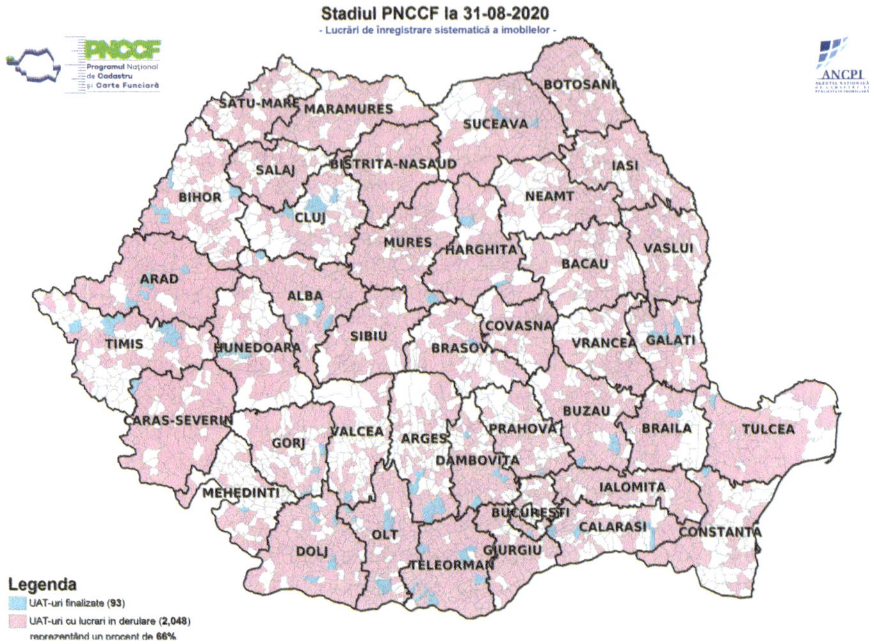

Fig. 5.13 Stage of implementation of the National Program for Cadastre and Land Registration Source: ANCPI, August 2020, http://www.ancpi.ro/files/Statistici_home_page/H3-Lucrari_de_inregistrare_sistematica_a_imobilelor_31.08.2020.pdf (date of access: September 24, 2020). Note: The map marks in light blue territorial administrative units with finalised cadastre projects and in purple territorial administrative units with projects in the course of implementation.

> You're right madam, we took nothing from PNDL II, we submitted a project on upgrading the streets, we received no written explanation, we used a consultancy company for submitting the project. We submitted it afterwards on FDI [Fund for Development and Investments].[24] (Mayoralty representative, Centre Development Region)

4. problems related to geographical demarcation—cadastre registration, which resulted in some cases in eligibility issues as previously identified also for European-funded projects (Marin, 2016). At the same time, the national project on cadastre registered delays in implementation (Fig. 5.13); therefore, there has not been a timely support from this large scale project, at least for part of the rural municipalities with registration issues impeding the projects' submission. Just as a reminder, the national agency (ANCPI) running the national level program on cadastre and land registration is an institution subordinated to the same Ministry running PNDL II—MLDPA, former MDRAP (Fig. 3.1). The latest updates (August 2020) from this institution show that the works have been finalised for only 93 territorial administrative units while for 2048, the

[24] Administered by the National Commission for Strategies and Prognosis—http://www.cnp.ro/ro/fonduldezvoltareinvestitii (date of access: August 20, 2020).

works are in the course of implementation. Furthermore, lack of stability or high dynamism in the regulatory framework or in human resources management has been mentioned among bottlenecks in funds' accession.

> We have nothing here with the national project on cadastre, we have two cadastre districts, we have bounded properties, but people have property titles since the '20s, with other standards and measurements than today, and this is why there still are unclarified items. I give you only one example – County Commission of Land, the files we submitted in 2016 are still not analysed. There is also a lack of political stability, prefects are changing, there are misunderstandings between the Forestry Directorate, Romsilva,[25] tensions that occurred, and all these resulted in a rhythm which is not normal ... There are also so many and frequent changes that we compile a documentation playing by the current rules of game, and then the rules change, and it results that we have to restore the documentation. (Mayoralty representative, North-West development region)

> We also have problems with the cadastre, but the national project on cadastre funded by European funds doesn't help us too much because executing companies are hard to find, the price is too low, we are in a mountain area here, and the price is more appropriate for the field, maybe there they also manage with the drones, but here it is not possible otherwise than on foot. (Mayoralty representative, West development region)

5. problems related to lack of transparency—county and local representatives recommended that the results of all submitted projects are publicly displayed. There have been cases where one territorial administrative unit submitted four projects, out of which two have been approved and no explanation provided for the remaining two. Some local leaders even projected that eventually, their projects would be approved, like in the example provided below. Their assumption is based on a future redistribution of funds within the program. Yet, the uncertainty of the funding environment remains high, according to the expressed perceptions. Only as a reminder, please note that the complete list of projects at a county level, for example, in Caraş-Severin, states that two project proposals would be funded through 'redistribution of funds' from PNDL (as mentioned in Sect. 3.4). Uncertainty can only be decreased by improved program transparency, especially in the phase of projects' selection.

> We submitted another project on PNDL II on pavement in our town, but it hasn't been approved; no, we received no explanation, we thought that it's maybe because they would give us too much money, and then, if you come to think about it, you first make the water investments [approved from PNDL II] and only after that, you make the road pavements [not approved from PNDL II] ...
>
> Then I start to think that from the sums not spent on this program, because it's one thing what you technically project as a sum, then at the procurement, there is another sum, this means there are unspent sums, and maybe some projects could be funded from them. (Mayor, North-West development region)
>
> We also submitted projects on water and sewerage, but it's quite difficult in our case because the villages are scattered, the houses are scattered as well, we are trying other solutions such as septic tanks.... Only recently we have one project on upgrading the streets; this is another project, not the one submitted on PNDL II. Otherwise, we

[25] Romsilva—National Agency of Forests (Regia Nationala a Padurilor).

> don't have any other project approved, we think that they should take into consideration people's needs, not the political affiliation. Funds' allocation is based on political affiliation, if the mayor goes or not in the ruling party, there was nothing said when the project had been rejected. (Mayoralty representative, Centre Development Region)

6. substantial differences between European and State Budget funds, both concerning the submission of projects as well as implementation phases. The 'competition' concerning time of implementation is, according to the expressed opinions, in favour of PNDL II, compared to European-funded projects. In relation to the first session of project submission from PNDL, the public institutions' representatives talked about paper-based submission of projects on PNDL II, in contrast with online applications on European funds.

> On PNDL II, from the moment you have the feasibility study ready and all the necessary certificates, then you proceed with signing the funding contract. Whereas on AFIR [Agency for Funding Rural Investments - European funds], from the moment you submit the funding proposal with everything you need, I have two sport facilities from two schools, I have received the notification that the documentation has been received, and I am waiting for three months to call me to sign the contract ....
>
> I am the living proof, madam. I started with European funds, and I also have projects on PNDL II, I am almost ready with them, 90% ready on PNDL II, works are almost ready and through European funds, I didn't even succeed to dig a hole. (Mayoralty representative, West development region)
>
> By that time at PNDL II project applications could not be submitted online, we took the files with all the papers and submitted them at the Ministry's Registry. After we submitted the projects, they asked from us all sorts of additions, and we answered them. I had large projects – three on roads and two on water and sewerage, we personally submitted them, all mayors stayed there in a queue at the Ministry's Registry. (Mayoralty representative, West development region)

7. a sufficient level of financial resources able to be mobilised quickly, as the opportunities on other funding lines like the European ones become available for communes or small urban areas. This becomes increasingly important, in particular for small and poor territorial administrative units that are not likely to be able to quickly grasp the funding opportunities on European funds.

> I am looking at my neighbours, South Siliştea, they moved out very quickly, they have been on Axis 13.1,[26] they found out about this on time and succeeded in finalising a large project.
>
> What does it mean they found out on time?
>
> It means they have been able to enter a contractual relationship with a consultancy company by the time the call has been launched, they had enough resources to mobilise teams able to work out the documentation. (Mayoralty representative, North-West development region)

8. interviewed representatives stated there was no specific support received from the County Council, besides meetings on information about available funds, mostly organised at the beginning of the programming period. Nonetheless, findings from the qualitative research on the financial support for co-financing

[26]The Specific Objective 13.1 from the Regional Operational Program targets improvement of people's quality of life in small and medium sized towns from Romania and supports improvement of social, educational and cultural-leisure services as well as improvement of urban public spaces.

the submitted projects should be regarded within the context of local financial capacity.

> County Council did not help us with anything; on the contrary, I tell you, on the contrary, they almost killed us with building permits. The County Council did not help with co-funding part, but we are the largest commune from the whole county, we have a larger budget when compared to other communes. (Mayoralty representative, West development region)

> But the invoices are very much delayed at the present time; we even had an invoice from the eleven month – paid in the month of May, I tell you frankly that I was ashamed to answer on the phone from the company, I didn't know what to tell them anymore. We submitted two projects, and both of them were approved; therefore, we say that it was a fair project, we haven't been disadvantaged, we have been in great need about the two projects submitted on PNDL II. The County Council did not help us with the co-funding part, but we also had some funds, because you know that many times a poor family has even more than a rich family. (Mayoralty representative, South East development region)

9. problems related to inter-institutional collaboration and lack of legislative stability.

> Issuing a Governmental Decision – the documentation started in 2017 and is related to a certain ministerial order from that date. At the beginning of September 2019, other norms were issued, and another ministerial order changing the rules of the game was issued. This order includes lots of factors that are not clearly defined, they leave room for interpretation and discussion; this means that a civil servant who wants to avoid doing something, sends you back the paper, and a lot of time is wasted. This means that one Governmental Decision takes unlawfully lot of time. I have been waiting for eight years for a Governmental Decision to be issued and transfer the building of the old treasury; it has been snowing and raining for seven years on that building. (Mayoralty representative, North-West development region)

10. problems related to a lack of specialised personnel or specialised consultancy companies from particular rural areas. Previous research (Marin, 2020) conducted on a sample of rural municipalities absorbing European funds in the period of 2009–2012 shows that working with specialised consultancy companies increases the municipality's likelihood of a developed absorption capacity. In the cited work, the municipality's absorption capacity is the number of approved projects benefiting from European funds in the period 2009–2012.

> some mayors from the rural area lack specialised personnel or specialised consultancy companies are missing from that area. (County Council representative, West development region).

To conclude, rural municipalities operate in different funding environments depending on the locality or county characteristics and other local level features. All these, together with structural eligibility criteria result in narrowing down the set of available funding lines and, thus, in choosing a particular organisational environment, at least for a part of rural municipalities. Enablers for their local development are useful to be taken into consideration whenever planning funds' allocation from the principals' level, usually represented by Ministries.

Are Rural Marginalised Areas Marginalised From Allocating PNDL Funds?

This study uses the definition of marginalised areas as identified through the study 'The Atlas of Rural Marginalized Areas and of Local Human Development in Romania' (Teşliuc et al., 2016). This means that three criteria of marginalisation are taken into consideration, related to: (1) human capital—proportion of population aged 15–64 years old that completed eight grades or less; (2) employment—proportion of people aged 15–64 years old neither in education nor have ever been in formal employment (employees, employers or pensioners), and (3) housing—proportion of dwellings not connected to electricity; proportion of overcrowded dwellings and proportion of dwellings not connected to piped water. By definition, marginalised areas refer to the rural census sectors that are disadvantaged in all three criteria (Teşliuc et al., 2016, 22). As can be noticed, the human capital and employment criteria were measured based on one key indicator each. A value higher than the threshold on the corresponding indicator qualified that census sector as being 'disadvantaged' in those criteria. In addition, the housing criterion was passed if any of the three key indicators was higher than its corresponding threshold.

At the national level, the same study identifies the following:

- 6.2% of the rural population, 5.3% of all households, and 5.2% of all dwellings are located in rural marginalised areas,
- in total, rural marginalised communities are spread across 992 communes (35% of all communes in the country),
- only 1605 villages in the country have one or more marginalised areas (census sectors)
- there are considerable differences at a county and regional level. Vaslui has the highest rate of rural marginalisation in the country, followed by other counties with high rates of rural marginalization, namely Iaşi, Covasna, Braşov, Botoşani, Galaţi, Bacău, Sibiu, and Mehedinţi.
- From the point of view of public infrastructure, marginalised areas tend to have, in a significantly larger extent, unpaved streets and bad housing and are exposed to environmental hazards (such as floods and landslides) and have poor quality or no public services (ibid.).

These characteristics show significant needs for investments in public infrastructure, similar to the investment objectives funded by PNDL—roads, bridges, water, sewerage, schools, kindergartens, dispensaries, etc. This section investigates whether allocations from PNDL II have targeted rural marginalised areas or not. In order to do this, the first step has been to identify the investment objectives at a more disaggregated level, that is, at a village level.

The entire database of local level investments funded from PNDL and included in this analysis comprises 6323 cases. Out of all these investments, most of them are located in the rural area—more precisely, 85% of all investment objectives have been awarded to rural localities, which accounts for 5379 cases of investment projects (Fig. 5.14). From all these investments located in the rural area, a case-by-

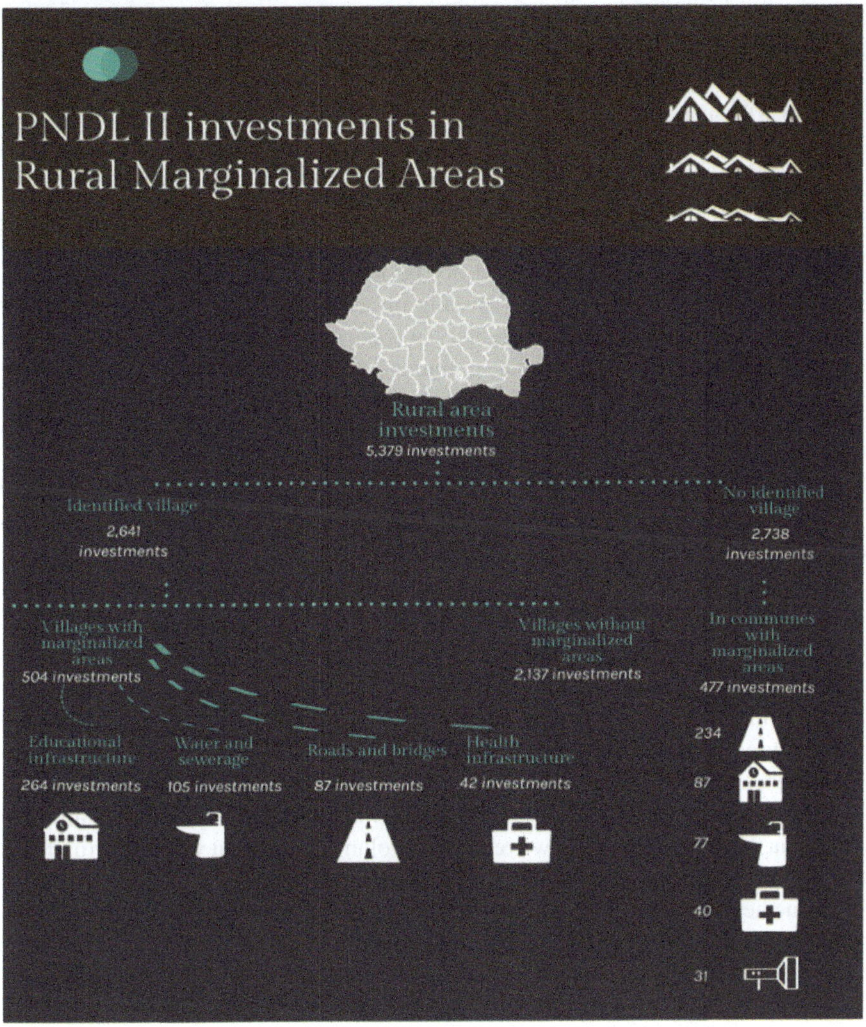

Fig. 5.14 Distribution of investments in marginalised areas at commune and village level. Data: author's calculations based on PNDL II list of investments database and data on rural marginalised areas provided in Teşliuc et al. (2016). Note: the rest of investments located in villages with marginalised areas includes six investments of other types and the rest of investments located in communes with marginalised areas includes eight other types of investments

case analysis tracked down the villages where the projects are placed in 2641 cases of projects. From all these identified cases, about 80% do not include marginalised areas. This means that, at village level, only a small part, about 17% of the investment projects, are in different types of rural marginalised areas, most part in rural marginalised areas with no households with self-identified Roma.

For the part of projects placed in villages with marginalised areas, most of them are about investments in educational infrastructure (264 projects), water and sewerage (105 projects) and roads and bridges (87 projects). Only 42 projects from villages with marginalised areas are about health infrastructure—dispensaries. Yet, this should be viewed in the general context of the entire locality (commune), where the dispensary (or office of the general practitioner) is placed in the central village ('sat centru de comună').

Nonetheless, there are also projects located in communes with marginalised areas, where the exact village could not be identified. This lack of village identification can be caused by either missing information, or by the typology of the investment, as is the case with water and sewerage (which can be prioritised/planned at a county level, not only at the commune level), or with investments in the main road from the village (which crosses most likely various villages from the commune). This is the case of 477 projects, out of which 234 projects are for roads and bridges, water and sewerage (77 projects), 87 projects are for educational infrastructure, 40 projects are for health infrastructure, 31 projects are for public lighting, and 8 projects are for other type of investments. They are potentially beneficial for all inhabitants of the commune.

We now take a closer look at the volumes of funds allocated to rural marginalised areas. In order to adopt a larger perspective on this issue, for the reasons mentioned above, we will take into consideration volumes of projects located in communes with marginalised areas, irrespective if the exact village has been clearly identified or not. This type of analysis shows that only a small share has been allocated for the analysed type of communes. In total, communes with marginalised areas have been allocated projects summing up to less than a quarter, more precisely about 20% of the total volume of funds directed towards all the rural municipalities in Romania through PNDL II. If we report this volume to the total volume of funds for municipalities, this share amounts to 17% of the total sum.

Nonetheless, it goes without saying that an enlarged perspective on the available funding opportunities for communes with rural marginalised areas should also take into consideration other funding lines. Another fact to be taken into consideration is that these areas accumulate several disadvantages on multiple dimensions. As previously mentioned in the work conducted on the relationship between public organisations and funding environment, there are also differences in risk preferences which might be related to the type of projects the agents are mostly willing to perform. Usually, projects in these areas require integrated interventions in which infrastructure improvement is only a part. Anyhow, the picture should be enlarged by taking into consideration if the corresponding commune has actually applied to PNDL II, with interventions located in the rural marginalised areas. Yet, this picture can only be made available if the principal (MDRAP) decides to adopt a more transparent manner of funds' allocation to the agents' level, with a clear identification of project localisation at a village level.

At this point in the analysis, there is a need to make clearer the distinction between projects/investments and the number of villages with marginalised areas where these investments are located. One project can be placed in one or more villages. One project can include various type of investments, for instance, water and sewerage are usually together in one project. Simultaneously, it can also be the case where the same location, for instance, a secondary school from a marginalised area, benefits from investments from three different projects. As an example, one can mention the case of Vulcan secondary school (Vulcan commune, Brasov county), where one project targets central heating, one investment is for repairing the roof, and one project is for extending the building. Consequently, three projects or investment objectives are located in the same building, one village. At a national level, this means that the 504 investments located in marginalised areas are placed in 624 villages, out of which 338 in rural marginalised areas with no self-identified Roma, 100 are in rural marginalised areas with less than 20% self-identified Roma, and 186 villages include rural marginalised areas with more than 20% self-identified Roma. In total, villages with marginalised areas covered by PNDL II investments (no matter which type of investment) account for 18% of all villages (identified) within the complete list of projects analysed in the rural area by this study.

At a county level, there are some clear discrepancies between the villages with marginalised areas covered by PNDL II investments. The largest number of villages with marginalised area per county are placed in Vaslui (94 villages), Iaşi (63 villages) and Botoşani (55 villages). These counties are among the counties identified with the highest rates of rural marginalisation in the country, as previously mentioned. By contrast, if we consider only the villages identified in the complete list of investments, Hunedoara and Prahova counties do not include any village with marginalised area.

In addition, the analysis of the investments in marginalised areas shows no investment for public lighting funded by PNDL II. This is, of course, true for the 2641 investments in which the village could be identified. This finding points out the need to increase the quality of life of the population living in these areas, including the perceived degree of public safety, by also investing in public lighting systems. Of course, it is not yet clear, at village level, how many of them already have public lighting systems.

As a concluding remark, only a small share of the volume of funds from PNDL II has been allocated to communes with rural marginalised areas, despite the urgent and extensive need to invest in an upgraded road and social infrastructure in these areas.

Chapter 6
Update 2020: Has Anything Changed in Between?

This study analysed the first allocations within PNDL II program, with an improved or at least changed formula of allocation, compared to the first part of the program, namely the first phase of the program PNDL I 2013–2020. The contracts analysed have been awarded until May 2018, with most of them allocated in the last months of 2017. Meanwhile, the Ministry of Regional Development and Public Administration has granted several other allocations from the same program. The following figure shows the evolution of allocations in the period of 2017–2020, according to the latest data published by the Ministry (presently the Ministry of Public Works, Development and Administration) in February 2020.[1]

The Ministry states that 'at the present time the contracting procedure for PNDL II—Second phase is underway, with a share of 98.32% of the total number of 7269 of objectives included in PNDL II'. This means, on the one hand, that there is a fixed number of objectives included in PNDL II and, on the other hand, that not all of them are with funded contracts at the present time. The problem that there is a fixed number of objectives included, yet they are not published (until funded) raises, again, issues of transparency and accountability from the part of the Ministry. The total number of contracts funded by February 2020 is 7142 contracts (total number of contracts represented in Fig. 6.1), which equals the share stated in the information from the Ministry, of 98.32%. Hence, if we consider the total number of contracts included in the analysis of the present study, based on the list of investment objectives by May 2018, this analysis covers 93% of all funding contracts in this program (Fig. 6.1).

The same source of information (data updated in February 2020) states that the total volume of funds allocated in PNDL II is almost double than in PNDL I. It also presents the following distribution by investment objective for the total sum approved, which means for all the contracts signed between 2017–2019 (Table 6.1). It shows that:

[1] Available at: https://www.mdrap.ro/lucrari-publice/pndl (date of access: March 26, 2020).

A. M. Marin, *Assessing PNDL*, https://doi.org/10.1007/978-3-030-82844-8_6

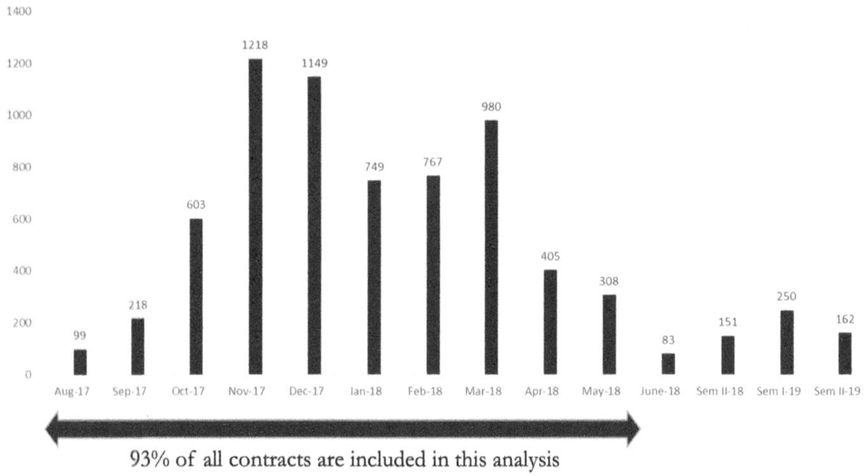

Fig. 6.1 Distribution of signed funded contracts in PNDL II by month in the period of 2017–2019. Source: Data published by the Ministry of Public Works, Development and Administration, as part of the PowerPoint presentation PNDL. Stage of implementation as of February 2020, available at: https://www.mdrap.ro/lucrari-publice/pndl (date of access: March 26, 2020)

- Only a small part (30%) of the total funds of the State Budget allocations for the entire period has been 'approved'—the total sum approved for 2017–2019, mentioned in the second column of Table 6.1.
- Most funds approved for PNDL II are for roads (52%) and water supply and sewerage (26%). Only a small part is for all types of educational units (schools, high schools, nurseries and kindergartens). Bridges and culverts, on the one hand, and health units, on the other hand, have the same share in the total funds approved for PNDL II between 2017–2019, of 4% each. Other fields, like public institutions, cultural objectives and touristic infrastructure, are only 2%.
- To sum up, the distribution of funds by investment objective is similar to the one identified in the previous analysis, taking into consideration all the contracts signed by May 2018.

Another point of update in this analysis has been to identify whether the territorial administrative units (rural/ urban municipalities and county councils) identified by this study as white marks' are still without funds from this program by the latest update of information available from central public administration institutions. For this purpose, a case-by-case analysis has been conducted in February-March 2020 in order to identify the new contracts signed for the municipalities or county councils which have been previously marked as 'white spots' on the map of funds analysed so far from the contracts awarded by May 2018 (Fig. 6.2). For this purpose, the latest update of information with all the contracts signed has been taken into consideration as the one available on Ministry's website for the month of November 2018.

Table 6.1 Funds and reimbursements from PNDL II up to February 2020

Field of investment	State budget allocations State budget	Total sum approved 2017–2019	Of which reimbursed 2019–Feb. 2020	Number of investment objectives 2017–2020	Number of investment objectives received
Water supply	2,246,958,809.62	808,127,232.87	265,763,263.58	546	50
Water supply + sewerage (integrated projects)	2,301,957,668.96	486,160,435.43	187,987,145.34	253	13
Sewerage	4,082,261,629.32	1,066,736,108.59	353,087,904.74	522	44
Roads	14,761,566,693.54	4,672,521.78259	1,401,071,096.43	2138	254
Education units, of which:	2,442,063,684.38	731,008,946.41	220,669,075.89	1401	213
Education units*	964,169,702.90	267,567,317.06	87,422,741.56	601	104
Education units* without operating permits	1,477,893,981.48	463,441,629.35	133,246,334.33	800	109
Nurseries and kindergartens	1,167,153,272.19	357,307,689.70	107,005,154.67	860	85
Health units	1,085,599,004.34	314,739,932.16	67,423,055.93	596	63
Bridges and culverts	1,134,312,483.61	352,555,288.47	104,268,837.11	456	60
Other fields**	456,392,007.70	138,907,962.11	45,238,287.52	497	146
TOTAL	29,678,265,253.66	8,928,065,378.33	2,752,513,821.21	7,269	928

Source: Data published by the Ministry of Public Works, Development and Administration, as part of the PowerPoint presentation PNDL. Stage of implementation as of February 2020, available at: https://www.mdrap.ro/lucrari-publice/pndl (date of access: March 26, 2020). Note: * primary schools, secondary schools and high schools, **—public institutions, cultural objectives, touristic infrastructure

At the municipality level, this analysis identified 295 cases of localities receiving no funds from PNDL II up to May 2018 (see the sub-section on General results for rural municipalities). Most of these are located in the rural area, more precisely 288 cases. Meanwhile, following the update of contracts up to November 2018, only 26 of these 295 cases of localities have been awarded contracts, with only one of them being allocated two contracts. This is the case for the communes of I.C.Brătianu (Tulcea county) and Valea Sării (Vrancea county). For the commune of I.C.Brătianu, from the county of Tulcea, one contract is for the municipality office ('setting up administrative office'), and one contract is for setting up pavements. In this respect, it is worth mentioning that the commune of I.C.Brătianu has been

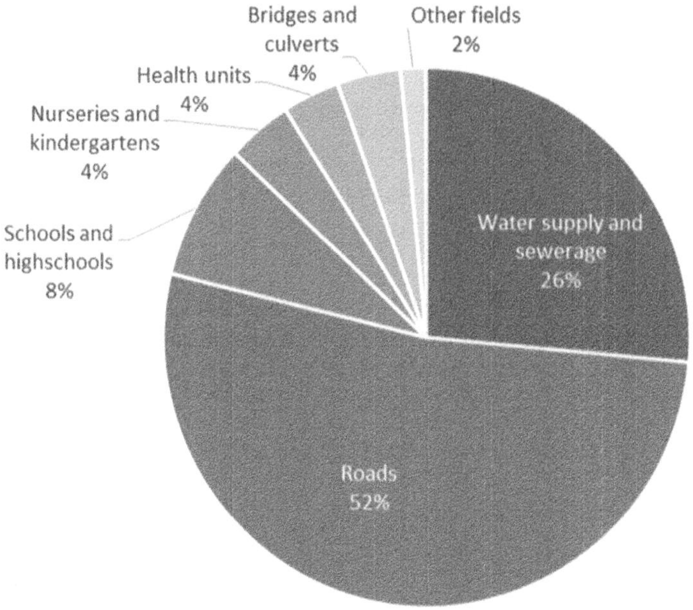

Fig. 6.2 Distribution by investment objective of the total funds approved for PNDL II between 2017–2019. Source: Data published by the Ministry of Public Works, Development and Administration, as part of the PowerPoint presentation PNDL. Stage of implementation as of February 2020, available at: https://www.mdrap.ro/lucrari-publice/pndl (date of access: March 26, 2020)

previously identified as amongst the ones in high need—low level of infrastructure and zero funds from either PNDL II or European funds (see Table 5.11). Yet, only more commune in a similar situation has received funding from PNDL II—Ciuperceni from Teleorman county. By similar situation, we refer to the list of communes mentioned in Table 5.11. Alike, it is difficult to say if they applied or not, in case there has been a public call for the remaining funds.

Furthermore, among the contracts listed in Table 6.2, one project stands out—Exhibition space of market for animals and Exhibition Market, in Viişoara, Cluj county. It is difficult to integrate it into one of the funding priorities mentioned by the Ministry in its response to the public information request. In the same county, Cuzdrioara has received funding for a multifunctional centre, most likely for social infrastructure, yet difficult to understand from the title.

In addition, only three cases from urban area (previously identified with zero funds absorption from PNDL II) have been awarded contracts in the following phases. These are represented by the towns of Borsec (Harghita county), Vişeu de Sus (Maramureş county) and Recaş (Timiş county). The complete list of contracts signed after May 2018 for the localities with zero funds absorption from PNDL II up to this date is presented below (Table 6.2). The total sum of these 'new' contracts amounts to 122,622,197 lei–27,249,377 euro, about 2% (of all allocations to urban and rural municipalities up to May 2018).

Table 6.2 List of contracts signed after May 2018 for the localities with zero funds absorption (Zero funds absorption considered until May 2018.) Source: Data published by the Ministry of Public Works, Development and Administration, as part of the PowerPoint presentation PNDL. Stage of implementation as of February 2020, available at: https://www.mdrap.ro/lucrari-publice/pndl (date of access: March 26, 2020)

County	SIRSUP	Locality	Area of residence	Sum of the contract	Type of investment
Alba	4106	Cilnic	rural	5,706,705	Sewerage
Arad	9743	Almaş	rural	1,322,190	Crossing bridge
Arad	9832	Archiş	rural	212,045	Pavements
Argeş	18,581	Comuna Săpata	rural	5,398,946	Roads
Buzau	48,138	Padina	rural	6,900,000	Roads
Caraş Severin	53,345	Naidăş	rural	6,039,952	Water and sewerage
Cluj	55,062	Cuzdrioara	rural	3,682,302	Multifunctional centre
Cluj	60,062	Viişoara	rural	515,126	Exhibition space of market for animals and Exhibition Market
Harghita	83,375	Păuleni Ciuc	rural	542,989	Public lighting
Harghita	83,491	Borsec	urban	1,622,700	Health unit (dispensary/ nursery)
Harghita	83,981	Ciucsângeorgiu	rural	1,177,235	Public lighting
Harghita	84,415	Frumoasa	rural	1,210,792	Roads
Harghita	84,923	Mărtiniş	rural	679,143	Roads
Harghita	85,074	Mihăileni	rural	1,241,159	Roads
Harghita	85,243	Ocland	rural	416,500	Bridge
Harghita	86,479	Leliceni	rural	558,558	Public lighting
Maramureş	106,979	Vişeu de Sus	urban	19,318,570	Roads
Mureş	119,466	Sînpaul	rural	3,535,249	Roads
Prahova	133,795	Izvoarele	rural	10,714,492	Roads
Sibiu	144,535	Cârţişoara	rural	2,995,880	Public lighting
Teleorman	151,709	Ciuperceni	rural	20,224,424	Roads
Teleorman	154,996	Nenciuleşti	rural	6,919,434	Roads
Timiş	158,314	Recaş	urban	5,914,634	Roads
Timiş	159,259	Vlad Delamarina	rural	5,710,050	Roads
Tulcea	161,525	I.C.Brătianu	rural	1,300,000	Pavements
Tulcea	161,525	I.C.Brătianu	rural	8,300,000	Administrative office
Vrancea	178,313	Valea Sării	rural	221,329	Roads
Vrancea	178,313	Valea Sării	rural	241,795	Roads

To conclude, this analysis covers most part of PNDL II allocation, and it largely remains relevant for the analysis of 'white spots' identified for 2018, communes and towns as well. It can thus serve as a solid basis to be further developed into an extended program evaluation.

Chapter 7
Update 2020: What Is the Relevance of Studying PNDL in the Context of the Global Crisis of COVID-19?

By the time this study has been finalised in February-March 2020, the outbreak of COVID-19 in Europe has started. Romania became part of this global crisis.[1] On March 16, 2020, an emergency state was enacted, as part of the health crisis due to COVID-19.[2]

There still are many issues left unknown in this global challenge. Most likely, countries with health systems performing poorly before this crisis will have even more obstacles to underpass during this timeframe. This is, for instance, the case of Romania.

From the point of view of investments funded through PNDL, there are two issues that can be of relevance. One of them is directly related to the investments in health infrastructure, and the other one is related to the investments in water and sewerage.

Investments in health infrastructure are particularly important as the current infrastructure in Romania is outdated, built in some cases 100 years ago, with intra-hospital circuit boards not functional at the present time (Ministry of Health, 2016). European funds did not succeed, up to the present time, in building three new regional hospitals, although such investments have been claimed to be achieved in the previous programming period. The investments funded from PNDL II program for the health infrastructure (medical dispensaries and hospitals) represent about 9% of the total number of investments included in this analysis (583 investments). By county, the largest number of investments in health infrastructure are located in the counties of Dâmboviţa (52 investments),[3] Iaţi (34 investments) and Suceava (31 investments). The investments in health infrastructure represent only 3% of the total funds allocated within PNDL II. Only a small number and, correspondingly, a low volume of funds is directed towards investments in health infrastructure in the urban area. About 85% of these investments are in rural area.

[1] Information in this section up to April 1st, 2020.

[2] Enacted by Presidential Decree no. 195/2020 on enactment of emergency state on Romania's territory.

[3] With a large number of school dispensaries in this county.

A. M. Marin, *Assessing PNDL*, https://doi.org/10.1007/978-3-030-82844-8_7

For instance, the funds directly related to health units could be used in the current health crisis. Investments in health units are particularly important in a country with the lowest level of funding as share from GDP in the European Union. Yet, in the absence of an integrated approach in the health system, this newly built infrastructure could be left unused. This is the case, for instance, of the Hospital from Mioveni. The estimated total cost for the Hospital from Mioveni, recently built, is of 68 million euro.[4] Just as a comparative overview, in 2015, the total sum allocated, in 2015, through European funds, for building three regional hospitals equals 150 million euro. They should have been ready built by 2020, but they are not. Their building has been postponed for the next programming period. In the database under analysis for this study, the municipality of Mioveni has three investment objectives, with a total sum of approximately 21 million euro. Other investment objectives funded from PNDL II for Mioveni relate to thermic rehabilitation of the buildings from a high school, building works for a kindergarten and building the urban hospital from Mioveni. The sum corresponding to this last objective amounts to 20 million euro in the database analysed by this study.

In March 2020, the County Committee for Emergency Situations (in Argeş county) decided that the Hospital from Mioveni should become a support hospital for tackling the COVID-19 crisis. After this decision at a county level, by the end of March, several physicians from Mioveni hospital resigned. The hospital manager declared that several physicians resigned but that their resignations have not been accepted. One of the main reasons is that 'it's difficult to start fighting with bare hands ... when you start fighting you need to know how many bullets you have ... we received some equipment, masks and some overalls which are not actually suited for this; this hospital has not been planned as an Infectious Diseases Hospital'.[5] On the other hand, the Prefect from Argeş stated that the County Committee for Emergency Situations decided that the Hospital from Mioveni will be a support hospital for COVID-19 cases and that the necessary certificates from Public Health Directorate were issued. 'We have no reason to change the decision. The equipment will come'.

Mioveni is not a singular case in this picture. Hospital managers and health staff from Suceava, Deva, Timişoara, Bucureşti, Braşov and Orăştie have also resigned in Romania during this global health crisis. It goes without saying that the COVID-19 crisis has hit unexpectedly even the most developed countries with high performing health systems, especially in the EU. The hospital from Mioveni, placed in a small urban area in Romania, although newly refurbished, is part of the global picture of a poorly performing national health system. Under these circumstances, investments in the health infrastructure do not guarantee an adequate response when faced with

[4]Source: https://www.digi24.ro/stiri/actualitate/sanatate/demisii-la-spitalul-mioveni-dupa-ce-s-a-decis-ca-unitatea-medicala-sa-trateze-pacienti-infectati-cu-coronavirus-1283294 (date of access: March 1st, 2020).

[5]Source: https://www.digi24.ro/stiri/actualitate/sanatate/demisii-la-spitalul-mioveni-dupa-ce-s-a-decis-ca-unitatea-medicala-sa-trateze-pacienti-infectati-cu-coronavirus-1283294 (date of access: March 1st, 2020).

the COVID-19 crisis. Nor do they guarantee an increase in the quality of the health system. It is about a country characterised[6] by a lower ratio of doctors and nurses per capita than most EU countries, the lowest health spending in the EU, a significant share of out-of-pocket payments, mostly for outpatient medicines, with only two development regions with a share of physicians per 1000 population higher than 3 (Bucharest-Ilfov and West regions). To add even more, Romania has a share of unmet needs (for medical care and for dental care) much higher and more unevenly distributed than the EU average.

Another issue related to the COVID-19 crisis is the compliance with the preventive hygiene measures, in particular related to the provisions of 'wash your hands frequently with water and soap'. From this perspective, this section examines the importance of investments in water and sewerage funded from PNDL II. Romania ranks last in the EU in what concerns population connected to public water supply,[7] with a share of 65.2% of the population, which means a lower share than that of Bosnia and Herzegovina, Albania or Serbia. Moreover, Romania ranks last in what concerns population connected to wastewater treatment plants,[8] yet better than Albania, Serbia, Bosnia and Herzegovina. Consequently, there is a great need to improve access to water and sewerage across Romania, especially in rural areas. In what concerns cosmetics and personal care consumption value in Europe 2018, Romania ranks a rather middle level position by country (million euro).[9] Yet, other indicators, such as the quantity of soap consumption per capita, would be also relevant considering the current context where importance of washing hands with soap and water has significantly increased.

In this respect, considering the importance of having running water at home, PNDL II funded an almost double number of investments in water and sewerage, when compared with the above-mentioned investments in health infrastructure. A large number of investments in water and wastewater treatments (above 100 investments per county) are placed in Argeş, Bihor, Dolj, Mureş, Olt, Prahova and Suceava. From this short list, only the counties of Dolj, Olt and Suceava have been pointed out as being part of the water supply sector access gap in Romania. These gaps are concentrated into two clusters—lower Danube (south) and the Moldavian and Ukrainian borders (northeast). The counties with the lowest water supply access rate are represented by Suceava, Botoşani and Vaslui and, in the lower Danube cluster the counties of Dolj, Olt, Teleorman, Giurgiu, Ilfov and Călăraşi

[6]Source: European Commission, OECD (2019) State of Health in the EU Romania Country Health Profile 2019, available at: https://www.oecd-ilibrary.org/docserver/f345b1db-en.pdf?expires=1586247189&id=id&accname=guest&checksum=864564CF782CD1BF4A685F7BE0997248.

[7]Code of the indicator: [env_wat_pop], Eurostat database, https://ec.europa.eu/eurostat/data/database (date of access: April 7, 2020).

[8]Code of the indicator: [env_ww_con], Eurostat database, https://ec.europa.eu/eurostat/data/database (date of access: April 7, 2020). For this indicator, the measure unit is share of population connected to sewer systems and wastewater treatment plants of resident population.

[9]https://www.statista.com/statistics/382100/european-cosmetics-market-volume-by-country/ (date of access: October 2, 2020).

(World Bank, 2018b, 140). Yet, in the study on improved prioritisation criteria for PNDL, there is a different ranking concerning water investment needs. According to this study, the highest investment needs in water infrastructure are placed in Iaşi, Argeş, Suceava, Timiş, Bacău, Prahova, Braşov and Mureş (Marteau et al., 2014: 262). Out of the most recent list (World Bank, 2018b), only the counties of Dolj, Olt, Suceava (more than 100 investments, as already mentioned), but also Teleorman (97 investments), Vaslui (86 investments) and Botoşani (78 investments) are among the top list of number of investments in water infrastructure. Yet, these data should be interpreted in the context of other potential funds—like the EU ones, the total sum of investments in water, the length of water supply and, most importantly, share of population/households connected to water supply within the community.

Here there is a need to make one special mention, particularly in regard to urban municipalities. Another relevant indicator for the water supply system is the share of streets with water distribution systems from the total length of streets. This indicator is related to the legislative provisions on the key minimum quantitative and qualitative indicators for defining urban localities—Annex II in Law no. 351/2001. In a similar manner, there is a reference to the share of streets with sewerage systems from the total length of streets. For the case of urban localities—the largest ones in Romania ('municipii'), the legal provisions state they should be 70% for water and, correspondingly, 60% for sewerage. For the smaller urban areas ('oraşe'), these shares are 60% for water and, respectively, 50% for sewerage. From this perspective, the analysis for urban municipalities shows that about 12% of urban municipalities (out of 312 urban municipalities for which data have been available) do not (yet) meet these legal provisions.

The total sum of funds invested in water infrastructure in the rural area from PNDL II shows a different hierarchy. If we look at results aggregated only for investments placed in the rural area, the top 10 includes a combination of priorities between the two lists mentioned above. The top 10 list of counties with the highest investment allocations in water infrastructure in the rural area includes the following counties (in descending order): Prahova, Dolj, Teleorman, Iaşi, Botoşani, Ialomiţa, Argeş, Suceava, Olt and Caraş Severin. This last county is not included in the funding priority by any study. At the bottom of the list, the last counties in funds allocation for water funded by PNDL II include Constanţa, Sibiu, Neamţ, Arad, Dâmboviţa, Covasna, Harghita, Ilfov, Giurgiu and Brăila, with the lowest volume of funds for water. From this list, only the county of Ilfov stands out as an 'outsider' of allocations for water, yet pointed out as a funding priority by the more recent WB study.

These investments in the total water supply infrastructure account for 35% of the total sum of funds analysed by this study as allocations in PNDL II. Out of the total number and funds allocated for water and sewerage infrastructure, more than 90% of investments and 92% of funds are for the municipalities in the rural area. At the level of county councils, PNDL only funded two investments in the counties of Dâmboviţa and Satu Mare. Alongside European funds as well as the funds allocated within the first stage of PNDL, they account for a major part of the funds for this sector. They could potentially contribute to, on the one hand, modernisation of the rural area and, on the other hand, of the most effective ways of saving illness or even lives in communities with a large share of elderly population, namely the most vulnerable group from the point of view of COVID-19 crisis. The funds from PNDL II support investments in this type of infrastructure, but the indicator under scrutiny is ultimately referring to the share of population connected to water and wastewater treatments. Even if effectiveness and impact under these terms exceed the scope of this study, the latest data available show that in the year 2018, the share of population connected in the urban area represents 89.5% of the urban resident population in Romania, whereas in the rural area, only 892,524 people benefited of sewerage services, which represents 9.9% of the total resident rural population in Romania.[10]

Previous WB study—Romania Water Diagnostic Report—highlights the need to improve access to water supply in rural Romania as a public health issue (World Bank, 2018b). The following conclusions of this study can be summed up here. They directly relate to the COVID-19 crisis as many cross-sectoral areas are of interest in this global crisis and its (potential) causes and consequences in Romania:

- The link between migration, rural areas and lack of access to water. Based on 2016 data, the study states that 4.5 million Romanians do not have access to piped potable water, mostly in rural areas affected by outmigration, and about half of these are relying on unsafe water sources (World Bank, 2018b, 130). The analysed rate of access in this study is even lower than in developing countries in Latin America and North Africa.
- There is no direct link between investments in the water supply infrastructure and the share of population connected to water supply, especially in rural Romania. This is mainly due to the increased risk of poverty in rural areas and the lack of a socially acceptable tariff in Romania.
- A long-term scenario, based on a ‘business as usual’ approach, shows that only the year 2040 would be a realistic target for Romania to achieve almost universal access to piped water and thus align with other EU countries (World Bank, 2018b, 256).
- To conclude, closing the piped water access gap should become a matter of national priority (World Bank, 2018b, 161).

All of these conclusions point out the need to integrate investments in the water infrastructure into the larger context of public health as well as poverty-related issues in order to increase the effectiveness of these investments. Nonetheless, the previous discussion on rural marginalised areas also shows the need to integrate access to public services in their renewal. But for this aim, more detailed data, at a village level, are needed.

[10]Source: National Institute of Statistics press release, June 2019, Population connected to sewerage and sewage treatment plants in the year of 2018, available at: https://insse.ro/cms/sites/default/files/com_presa/com_pdf/sistem_canal_2018r.pdf (date of access: April 8, 2020).

'Nowadays more people are very satisfied because they can connect to water and sewage; we would like to attract young population to come to us, but also elderly population. Now I need to tell you that this virus helped us a bit, because people returned to their parents' house so they would not stay isolated in a block of flats, and they have been very satisfied when they saw they can connect to water and sewage. I saw here in our commune people returning from the town, I haven't seen them since 2012, they preferred to come to their parents' house than stay in Bucharest. In our case, the distance is about 80–90 km away from Bucharest, and to me, it doesn't seem too far for the young people from Bucharest in case they want to come to us'. (Mayoralty representative, South development region)

Chapter 8
Conclusions and Recommendations

This book is about predictors of getting funds from Romania's largest State Budget funded program—the National Program for Local Development (PNDL). It aims to contribute to an objective assessment of the way State Budget funds from Romania's largest program are allocated at the level of county councils and municipalities in the urban and rural area. It covers allocations of the second phase of program implementation, namely the 'reformed one', PNDL II 2017–2020, with a double volume of funds than its previous phase.

Most of the debate around this program has been carried out more in the circle of politicians and less in that of scientific research. This study aims to fill in this gap by bringing in the spotlight a national level analysis on this topic, based on a secondary analysis of publicly available data. The analysis is differentiated against the three key levels of local public administration—county councils, urban and rural municipalities.

The study relies on a triangulation of data sources and methods to increase the robustness of findings and conclusions. Findings based on a secondary analysis of open data have been put in the larger settings of the Romanian system of public administration as a result of the extensive desk review and contextual analysis conducted. In addition, open data on PNDL II funding allocations published by the Ministry of Regional Development and Public Administration have been supplemented with relevant statistical information at locality level from the National Institute of Statistics, as well as local development indexes currently available—for rural localities, technical and building endowment index, together with the index of local human development. Moreover, various other indicators (mainly on own revenues and EU funds) from the database of local budgets execution as published by the specialised department from MDRAP—General Directorate of Public Administration, Directorate for Local Fiscal and Budgetary Policies have been used. Based on the desk review, additional data sources have been integrated into a common database. A case-by-case analysis has been performed for 5379 investment objectives placed in the rural area. This type of analysis has

A. M. Marin, *Assessing PNDL*, https://doi.org/10.1007/978-3-030-82844-8_8

been conducted in order to identify PNDL II funded investments located in rural marginalised areas, at a village level.

Additionally, the quantitative analyses carried out on the compiled databases have been complemented with the qualitative information collected through interviews conducted by phone in the period of December 2019–July 2020. In total, representatives of eleven public institutions from county, urban and rural levels expressed their opinions. The key topics included in the interview guide have been focused on the process of funds' allocation, main bottlenecks and issues encountered, support received and specific recommendations for improving program management. Stakeholders participating in the qualitative research represented local communities placed in different development regions of Romania, including cases of municipalities with maximum and minimum allocations from PNDL II.

PNDL is the largest State Budget funded program and has been reformed in the second stage of implementation, the one studied by this book. Besides studying and explaining maximum and minimum allocations at county, urban and rural levels from PNDL II, the book also brings about added knowledge with a comparative overview of the volume of funds with EU funds allocation at the level of territorial administrative unit (county or municipality); a detailed analysis of investment objectives at county, urban and rural municipality levels; a comprehensive analysis of the match between funds allocation in rural marginalised areas as well as an update of the relevance of the research for the new context in the global crisis of COVID-19.

Several explanatory models have been conducted for the three key levels of analysis—county, urban and rural municipalities. At a county level, a multiple regression model shows that the volume of PNDL funds at a county level depends indirectly on the volume of EU funds absorbed in the previous period. In other words, all other things being equal or held constant, a county council is more likely to have more funds from PNDL II as it has less population density and less developed absorption capacity of EU funds in the previous programming period, 2007–2013, meaning it is not in the upper quartile of EU funds absorption.

Additionally, at a county level a comparative analysis between absorbed EU and PNDL II funds shows a type of behaviour dependency. At agents' level, these results seem to be competitive in the sense that results for one system are achieved at the expense of another system. The recommended approach would be that these results are symbiotic, namely two systems are reciprocally dependent on each other's result (Marion, 1999).

For urban municipalities, a multiple regression model shows that, all other things being equal or held constant, an urban municipality is more likely to have more funds from PNDL II as it is less developed according to the human development index, it has fewer positions in the organisational size (based on the maximum number of available positions stated in the law), is located in a county with an experienced President of the County Council (more than 10 years in the position of County Council President), and it is within a county with less administrative units.

In a similar manner for the rural municipalities, a multiple regression model shows that, all other things being equal or held constant, a rural municipality is more likely to have more funds from PNDL II as it is less developed according to the human development index, its mayor has the same political affiliation as the ruling party, is located within South-East or South-West development regions, it has a population size under 3000 inhabitants, it has less developed infrastructure development, a smaller organisational size and is placed within a county with less administrative units.

Most of the local level investments from PNDL II are located in rural area. Nevertheless, a case-by-case analysis of every project from the rural area succeeded in identifying the village where the investment is located in only 49% of cases. Furthermore, out of the investments with an identified village, only a small part, about 17% of the investment projects, are in different types of rural marginalised areas, most part in rural marginalised areas with no household with self-identified Roma.

Given the large amount of time span for completing this analysis, another type of case-by-case analysis of projects has updated the information concerning the 'white marks' of territorial administrative units with an analysis of the contracts awarded in later funding sessions (up to February–March 2020). Therefore, this analysis identified whether this category of localities is still without funds from this program by the latest update of information available from central public administration institutions. At the municipality level, this analysis identified 295 cases of localities receiving no funds from PNDL II up to May 2018. Most of these are located in rural area, more precisely 288 cases. Meanwhile, only 26 of these 295 cases of localities have been awarded contracts, with only one of them being allocated two contracts. In addition, only three cases from urban area (previously identified with zero funds absorption from PNDL II) have been awarded contracts in the following phases. Therefore, the analysis of 'white spots' largely holds true for the present time.

Additionally, insights from the qualitative research conducted in the period of March–July 2020 revealed several problems for accessing funds from PNDL II for the case of 'white spots' but also broader problems, with impact on various local communities. Rural municipalities operate in different funding environments depending on the locality or county characteristics and other local level features. All these, together with structural eligibility criteria, result in narrowing down the set of available funding lines and, thus, in choosing a particular organisational environment, at least for a part of rural municipalities. Cases of asymmetric information between agents or adaptive leadership in the form of a process variable have been signalled. Problems related to cadastre registration, lack of transparency, poor financial and human resources, weak inter-institutional collaboration or lack of legislative stability have also been identified. Interviewed stakeholders signal in addition, substantial differences between European and State Budget funds, both concerning the submission of projects as well as implementation phases. The 'competition' concerning time of implementation is, according to the expressed opinions, in favour of PNDL II, compared to European-funded projects.

What Can Be (Better) Done Next?

At the level of decision-makers and representatives of central public administration, the prominent recommendation would be to increase the transparency of publicly available information. This can be achieved in multiple ways, yet one key variable should be included in the published files. This is the SIRUTA code as a unique identifier at the level of locality or county, or even village (SIRINF code works in a similar manner as a unique identifier at the village level). If this is achieved, then both transparency as well as coordination of investments can further improve.

This simple recommendation has already been enacted by other public institutions posting open data such as a subunit from the Ministry of Regional Development and Public Administration (General Directorate of Public Administration, Directorate for Local Fiscal and Budgetary Policies) publishing annually local budgets execution. Another example is offered by the Central Electoral Bureau publishing results in the local elections. Information from both sources has been used in this study.

In terms of issues left for further research, future studies might address:

- Enlarged complementary information gathered with the support of qualitative methods to encompass the subjective view of mayors of rural and urban municipalities as well as representatives of the County Councils.
- A comparative overview with other post-communist countries can significantly increase the relevance of the research.
- An improved explanatory model for the rural mayoralties, with testing of other predictors that can account for a better share of the dependent variable variance.
- Objective investments funded through European funds added in a standardised database in order to refine the analysis at national level. Consequently, this would enable a comprehensive mapping at a locality or village level for all major investments conducted. This kind of detailed mapping would substantially contribute to both horizontal and vertical coordination of funding instruments, which would ensure coherent planning across levels of government.
- Extend the use of principal-agent theory to the analysis of the process of implementing PNDL II funding contracts.
- The comparative perspective between State Budget and European funds can be further elaborated by adding all sources of State Budget funds, with an update for the present time.

Additionally, interviewed stakeholders expressed several recommendations aimed to improve program management, as follows:

1. an improved transparency of the program, accompanied by prioritisation criteria and explicit publishing of the reasons for not selecting particular projects. This recommendation also applies to other State Budget funded programs like the ones promoted afterwards by the National Commission for Prognosis or any other

investment programs, such as those run by the National Company of Investments or the educational infrastructure program run by the Ministry of Education.

> the program should be maintained, the program is good, but prioritisation and selection should be improved, and the reason for not selecting a project should be published. It should be clearly written that it was not according to criterion 3.1., and within the selection criteria, some adapted procedures for particular cases should be included. (County Council representative, West development region)

2. improved legislation or eligibility criteria for localities in which the legal status of properties is not clear yet. Nonetheless, an unclear situation of the local land properties usually poses challenges in accessing any type of funding. In these cases, most likely, a synergetic and complementary action with the national project on cadastre will be mostly welcome.

> We wrongly started with property registration for natural persons instead of legal persons, and, due to a human error, measurement points are on the street, and now the physical limits of properties are on the street, and they are out of the street area. It takes a lot of time and only one street costs about 1000 lei. On the national cadastre project, we are only at the outside built area land. This project moved rather difficultly at the national level because too little money has been awarded. (Mayoralty representative, South development region)

> Anyway, legislation should be simplified because particular cases do not succeed in being funded because part of the communes does not have clear property demarcation and registration, there is no clear legal status of the land, it is not clear on specific parts of the road and registration of land objectives. (County Council representative, West development region)

3. a publicly available database with projects, irrespective of their source of funding, grouped together under major topics: roads infrastructure, water and sewage, sewerage, public lighting, public institutions offices, etc. Such a type of database could work as a best practices exchange example between representatives of public institutions facing similar challenges. In this respect, MDRAP is placed in a very good position to elaborate and publish this database as it manages large and diverse projects from both European and State Budget funds.

> I think this is a very good idea, to have a database at a national level in which to see all the projects; for instance, if you want to build a water treatment system in which to see all the projects of this kind made before you. It should be publicly available online, and all the mayoralties and county councils should be able to access it as a best practice example and eventually have meetings with colleagues. I am working on projects on waste management, and in common meetings, I met colleagues and exchanged views, and it's very useful like this. (County Council representative, West development region)

In a nutshell, all these recommendations regard a transparent and coherent coordination of public investments, irrespective of the investment objective or funding line. Achieving this recommendation represents a prerequisite for better horizontal and vertical coordination instruments as well as an improved multi-level dialogue in order to set investment priorities.

> What else should be done on PNDL II? We no longer have a country strategy to know where to go, how my grandmother asked me 30 years ago: What do you want to be

when you grow up? This is also how our politicians should ask themselves, where do you want Romania to be after 30 years? We no longer have objectives as a country since 2007 when Romania was admitted in the EU. (Mayoralty representative, North-West development region)

Chapter 9
Annex

9.1 Annex 1. Public Information Requests Submitted to the Ministry of Regional Development and Public Administration

9.1.1 Annex 1.1. First Public Information Request Submitted to MDRAP

No. 37/ October 15, 2018

Public Information Request Based on Law No. 544/2001 on Free Access to Public Information

To:

Ministry of Regional Development and Public Administration

Bd. Libertăţii, no. 16, Latura Nord, sector 5, Bucureşti, postal code 050706

Dear Madam/ Sir,

Through this document, I would like to submit a request in line with Law no. 544/ 2001 on free access to public information requests. I would like to receive in electronic format the following information:

1. List of all funding requests received in the second phase of the Local Development National Program (PNDL) 2017–2020, including the following information:
   - Name of the territorial administrative unit (or of the intercommunity development association) as well as the corresponding SIRUTA code

A. M. Marin, *Assessing PNDL*, https://doi.org/10.1007/978-3-030-82844-8_9

- Name of the investment objective
- Total sum requested for funding

2. List of criteria taken into consideration when assessing the funding requests received with the purpose of selecting investment objectives awarded with funds in the phase of PNDL 2017–2020.

I would like to receive the requested information, in electronic format, at the following e-mail address:.....

I would like to thank you in advance for your response. Respectfully,

9.1.2 Annex 1.2. Second Public Information Request Submitted to MDRAP

No. 38/ October 23, 2018

Public Information Request Based on Law No. 544/2001 on Free Access to Public Information

To:

Ministry of Regional Development and Public Administration

Bd. Libertăţii, no. 16, Latura Nord, sector 5, Bucureşti, postal code 050706

Dear Madam/ Sir,

Through this document, I would like to submit a request in line with Law no. 544/ 2001 on free access to public information requests. I would like to receive in electronic format the following information:

1. List of all funding requests received in the second phase of the Local Development National Program (PNDL) 2017–2020, including the following information:
    - Name of the territorial administrative unit (or of the intercommunity development association) as well as the corresponding SIRUTA code
    - Name of the investment objective
    - Total sum requested for funding
2. List of criteria taken into consideration when assessing the funding requests received with the purpose of selecting investment objectives awarded with funds in the phase of PNDL 2017–2020.

I would like to point out that this is in regard to the total sum of 13,097 funding requests issued for eligible objectives mentioned in the answer[1] submitted by your

[1] Or in presenting the stage of PNDL implementation as of September 15, 2018, http://www.mdrap.ro/lucrari-publice/pndl.

institution in response to the public information request no. 119307/19.10.2018, following the public information request registered to the Information Point no. 119307/15.10.2018, and in the Registry for registering requests and answers to public information access and for managing the process of access to public information with the number of S 2234/15.10.2018. These information have been requested to your institution also in the previously mentioned request.

I would like to receive the requested information, in electronic format, at the following e-mail address: ...

I would like to thank you in advance for your response. Respectfully.

9.1.3 Annex 1.3. MDRAP's Response to the Second Public Information Request Submitted

Dear Madam/ Sir,

Regarding your request, sent to the Ministry of Regional Development and Public Administration (MDRAP) to the address info@mdrap.ro and registered with the no. 122985/23.10.2019 regarding the total number of over 13,000 eligible requests registered at the beginning of the second phase of National Program of Local Development (PNDL), approved by OUG no. 28/2013, with all the subsequent changes and additions, we communicate the following:

Data you requested are those that have been previously communicated, by the address no. 119307/19.10.2018. Public information on PNDL implementation is available on Ministry's website—www.mdrap.ro.

Requests for inclusion in the program are not part of public information documents category of MDRAP, because they are issued by local public authorities.

According to art.2, letter b from Law no. 544/2001, on free access to public information, with all the subsequent changes and additions, public information request means any information regarding activities or results from activities of a public authority or institution, no matter the support, the form or the way for expressing the information.

Faithfully,

9.2 Annex 2. List of Variables Included in the Analysis

Variables	Operationalization	Data source	Level of analysis
Fiscal capacity—own revenues in total revenues (2017) (%)/ own revenues per inhabitant	Own revenues are computed based on the indicator named 'own revenues' in the local budgets execution database minus the sums deducted from the personal income tax, in order to include only the sums upon which local public authorities have the largest degree of autonomy	General directorate of public administration, Directorate for local fiscal and budgetary policies, ministry of regional development and public administration, Annex 24. Revenues and expenditures for territorial administrative units, available at: http://www.dpfbl.mdrap.ro/sit_ven_si_chelt_uat.html	County councils Urban and Rural municipalities
Winners of EU funding 2007–2013	Local public authorities in the upper quartile of EU funding, based on the local budgets execution database (budgetary code 56: projects with non-reimbursable external funding). The indicators are computed as sum of volumes of funds absorbed in the period of 2009–2017, corresponding to the budgetary programming period of 2007–2013	General directorate of public administration, Directorate for local fiscal and budgetary policies, ministry of regional development and public administration, Annex 24. Revenues and expenditures for territorial administrative units, available at: http://www.dpfbl.mdrap.ro/sit_ven_si_chelt_uat.ht	County councils Urban and Rural municipalities
Population	County/locality population as registered in the population census of 2011	National institute of statistics, census results, available at: http://www.recensamantromania.ro/rezultate-2/	County councils Urban and Rural municipalities
Political affiliation of county council's president	President's political affiliation, binary variable according to the official data provided. Codifications of political affiliation included in the analysis for urban and rural municipalities include a binary variable which codes with 1 if the mayor belongs to PSD, (ruling party), ALDE or UDMR (support for the ruling party). In January 2018, UDMR voted in favour of a new government formed by PSD and ALDE	Data from the Central electoral office, local elections of 2016, available at: http://www.2016bec.ro/rezultate-finale-10-06-2016/index.html	County councils

(continued)

Variables	Operationalization	Data source	Level of analysis
Experience of county council's president	Experience as president of the county council, binary variable, 1-equal or more than 10 years experience as president of the county council, 0—less than 10 years experience as president of the county council	Data from county councils' websites, accessed online in December 2018–January 2019	County councils
Size of the budget	Level of expenditures for 2017	General directorate of public administration, Directorate for local fiscal and budgetary policies, ministry of regional development and public administration, Annex 24. Revenues and expenditures for territorial administrative units, available at: http://www.dpfbl.mdrap.ro/echilibrare_initiala.html	County councils
County area	County Area (ha)—building land area as displayed in the official data published by the ministry of regional development and public administration. This indicator is also used in the equalisation grants formula, as provisioned by the Law no. 273/2006 on local public finances	General directorate of public administration, Directorate for local fiscal and budgetary policies, ministry of regional development and public administration, initial equalisation data, available at:http://www.dpfbl.mdrap.ro/echilibrare_initiala.html	County councils Urban and Rural municipalities
Early starters of EU funding 2014–2020	County councils that succeeded in starting implementation of EU funded projects from the programming period of 2014–2020. The indicator considers as early starters those county councils that reported expenditures (greater than zero) in the budgetary execution for the budgetary code no. 58—projects with non-reimbursable external funding for the period of 2014–2020. These expenditures are reported for the budgetary executions of 2016 and 2017	General directorate of public administration, Directorate for local fiscal and budgetary policies, ministry of regional development and public administration, Annex 24. Revenues and expenditures for territorial administrative units, available at: http://www.dpfbl.mdrap.ro/sit_ven_si_chelt_uat.html	County councils Urban and Rural municipalities

(continued)

Variables	Operationalization	Data source	Level of analysis
Share of modernised county/ urban roads in the total length of county roads	Indicator computed as the ratio between the length of modernised county roads within the total length of county roads. Data are extracted from the NIS publication	Data at county level are extracted from the publication of the National Institute of Statistics (2018) Length of transport ways at the end of 2017, available at: http://www.insse.ro/old/sites/default/files/field/publicatii/lungimea_cailor_de_transport_la_sfarsitul_anului_2017.pdf	County councils Urban municipalities
		Data for the urban municipalities are extracted from the National Institute of Statistics—Tempo online database. Codes of the indicators—GOS104A—Length of urban roads by counties and localities and GOS105A—Length of modernised urban roads by county and locality, available online at: http://statistici.insse.ro:8077/tempo-online/#/pages/tables/insse-table	
Population density	Population/area	Computed based on population and building land area as detailed above	
Local human development index by Counties (2011)	The index of local human development (LHDI) measures the total capital of localities, especially in relation to four dimensions: human capital, health capital, vital capital and material capital. The methodology for computing this index is provided by professor Dumitru Sandu (2011), Disparitati sociale in dezvoltarea si in politica regionala din Romania. International Review of Social Research, I(1), 1–30	Data at county level are extracted from Marteau et al. (2014) Component 2, evaluation of the portfolio of regional development investments projects, prioritisation criteria for local infrastructure development projects, final report, p. 163	County councils Urban and Rural municipalities

(continued)

Variables	Operationalization	Data source	Level of analysis
Total length of the simple network of drinking water distribution, by counties and localities	Data are based on the statistical research on water supply, drainage, sanitation and thermic energy distribution	Data for the urban and rural municipalities are extracted from the national institute of statistics—Tempo online database. Code of the indicator—GOS106B—Total length of simple network of drinking water distribution, by counties and localities, available online at: http://statistici.insse.ro:8077/tempo-online/#/pages/tables/insse-table	Urban and rural municipalities
Part of a local action group	Urban and rural municipalities which are part of a local action group (GAL)	Data for urban and rural municipalities are extracted from the official information published by the ministry of agriculture and rural development—List of selected local action groups (January 2019), available at: http://www.madr.ro/docs/dezvoltare-rurala/Axa_LEADER/2014-2020/Lista_cu_Grupurile_de_Actiune_Locala_selectate_de_MADR_si_datele_de_contact_ale_acestora_actualizata_la_25.01.2019.pdf	
Infrastructure development—Technical and building endowment of the rural municipalities	Index composed in a study conducted by the academy of economic studies (2015), including the following indicators: (1) Share of dwellings connected to water supply in the total number of dwellings; (2) Share of dwellings connected to drainage in the total number of dwellings; (3 Share of dwellings connected to gas distribution network in the total number of dwellings; (4) Density of public roads network	Data for the rural municipalities are extracted from the study conducted by the academy of economic studies (2015), study on establishing the social and economic potential of rural areas development, pp.82–175, available at: http://www.madr.ro/docs/dezvoltare-rurala/programare-2014-2020/studiu-potential-socio-economic-de-dezvoltare-zone-rurale-ver-10.04.2015.pdf	Rural municipalities

(continued)

Variables	Operationalization	Data source	Level of analysis
Volume of funds absorbed through PNDL 2017–2020	Categories of volume of funds allocated for rural municipalities	Allocations by project/ projects are aggregated at the level of municipality. Allocations at project level are compiled according to the official information published by the ministry of regional development and public administration for PNDL II (stage of implementation as of May 1st, 2018, available here: http://www.mdrap.ro/lucrari-publice/pndl). Allocations at municipality level are transformed in Euro based on the annual average exchange rate published by the National Bank of Romania. For enabling comparison between municipalities, allocations in euro/ inhabitant are computed. Population data are the ones from the population census of 2011. Multiple regression analyses take into consideration total volume of funds absorbed through PNDL 2017–2020 (euro) per capita	
Mayor's political affiliation	Mayor's political affiliation, binary variable, 1-belongs to PSD (ruling party at the time of PNDL 2017–2020 decisions allocations), 0—does not belong to PSD	Data from the central electoral office, local elections of 2016, available at: http://www.2016bec.ro/rezultate-finale-10-06-2016/index.html	Localities
Rural marginalised areas		Data from the atlas of rural marginalised areas and of local human development in Romania (Teşliuc et al., 2016)	

References

Academy of Economic Studies in Bucharest (2015). *Study on establishing the socio-economic development potential of rural areas* (Studiu privind stabilirea potenţialului socio-economic de dezvoltare al zonelor rurale). Retrieved February 10, 2019 from http://www.madr.ro/docs/dezvoltare-rurala/programare-2014-2020/studiu-potential-socio-economic-zone-rurale.pdf

Addison, H. (2009). *Is administrative capacity a useful concept? Review of the application, meaning and observation of administrative capacity in political science literature*. London School of Economics and Political Science [Online]. Retrieved August 10, 2012 from http://personal.lse.ac.uk/addisonh/Papers/AC_Concept.pdf

Ahmad, E., & Martinez, L. (2004). *On the design and effectiveness of targeted expenditure programs*. IMF Working Paper No. 04/220. International Monetary Fund.

Aldrich, H., & Pfeffer, J. (1976). Environments of organizations. *Annual Review of Sociology, 2*, 79–105.

Andrews, R., & Boyne, G. (2010). Capacity, leadership and organizational performance: Testing the black box model of public management. *Public Administration Review, 70*(3), 443–454.

Astley, G., & Van de Ven, A. (1983). Central perspectives and debates in organization theory. *Administrative Science Quarterly, 28*(2), 245–273.

Bansal, P., & Gao, J. (2006). Building the future by looking to the past. Examining research published on organizations and environment. *Organization& Environment, 19*(4), 456–478.

Bezes, P. (2020). Seeing public bureaucracies like a sociologist: (A plea towards) reconnecting sociology and public administration. In J. Bouckaert (Ed.), *European perspectives for public administration: The way forward* (pp. 163–185). Retrieved August 10, 2012 from https://www.jstor.org/stable/j.ctvv417th.13

Brugha, R., & Varvaszovski, Z. (2020). Stakeholder analysis: A review. *Health Policy and Planning. Oxford University Press, 15*(3), 239–246.

Burduja, S., Ionescu Heroiu, M., Moţ, M., Moldovan, C., Rusu, R., Man, T., Gaman, F., Piontek, R., & Manea, M. M. (2015). Coordination of strategies and programs for EU and state-funded investments in romania's infrastructure. World Bank. Retrieved from February 7, 2019 https://openknowledge.worldbank.org/handle/10986/24455

Christensen, T., Lægreid, P., Roness, P., & Røvik, K. A. (2007). *Organization theory and the public sector.* New York: Routledge.

Council of Europe. (2014). Structure and operation report of local and regional democracy. Romania, February 2014. Retrieved February 1, 2019 from https://rm.coe.int/16807471c6

Dąbrowski, M. M. (2010). *Europeanisation of Polish regions: Impact of the European Union's structural funds on sub-national institutions and regional development policy practice*. Ph.D. Thesis. University of the West of Scotland.

A. M. Marin, *Assessing PNDL*, https://doi.org/10.1007/978-3-030-82844-8

Darby, J., Muscatelli, A., & Roy, G. (2003). Fiscal decentralisation in Europe: A review of recent experience. *European Research in Regional Science, 13*, 1–32. ISSN 0960-6130. Retrieved February 7, 2019 from https://strathprints.strath.ac.uk/6920/

de Oliveria, B. C., & Filho Fontes, R. J. (2017). Agency problems in the public sector: the role of mediators between central administration of city hall and executive bodies. *Brazilian Journal of Public Administration, 51*(4), 596–615.

Denters, B. (2011). Local governance. In M. Bevir (Ed.), *The SAGE handbook of governance* (pp. 313–330). Retrieved February 7, 2019 from http://dx.doi.org/10.4135/9781446200964

Doroftei, M., & Dimulescu, V. (2015). Corruption risks in the Romanian infrastructure sector. In A. Mungiu-Pippidi (Ed.), *Government favouritism in Europe. The anticorruption report* (vol. 3, pp. 19–34). Barbara Budrich Publishers.

Diaz-Cayeros, A., & Magaloni, B. (2003). The politics of public spending. Part I – The logic of vote buying. Retrieved February 7, 2019 from http://documents1.worldbank.org/curated/en/183571468758744201/pdf/269490v110Caye1s1of1public1spending.pdf

DiMaggio, P., & Powell, W. W. (1983). The iron cage revisited: Institutional isomorphism and collective rationality in organizational fields. *American Sociological Review, 48*(2), 147–160, (14 pages). Retrieved February 7, 2019 from https://www.jstor.org/stable/2095101?read-now=1&seq=10#page_scan_tab_contents

European Commission. (2016). The State of European Cities 2016. Cities leading the way to a better future. European Union, United Nations Human Settlements Programme (UN-Habitat). Retrieved February 7, 2019 from https://ec.europa.eu/regional_policy/sources/policy/themes/cities-report/state_eu_cities2016_en.pdf

European Commission, OECD. (2019). State of health in the EU Romania country health profile 2019. Retrieved February 7, 2019 from https://www.oecd-ilibrary.org/docserver/f345b1db-en.pdf?expires=1586247189&id=id&accname=guest&checksum=864564CF782CD1BF4A685F7BE0997248

Fazekas, M. (2014). *Prometheus unbound: Quality of government and institutionalized grand corruption in public procurement,* Ph.D. Dissertation. University of Cambridge, Department of Sociology.

Fiscal Council. (2019). Fiscal council opinion regarding state budget law, social insurances budget for the year of 2019 and fiscal budgetary strategy for the period of 2019–2021. Retrieved February 7, 2020 from http://www.consiliulfiscal.ro/Opinie%20CF%20buget%202019.pdf

Fiscal Council. (2020). Annual report for 2019. Retrieved June 7, 2020 from http://www.consiliulfiscal.ro/RA%20CF%202019.pdf

Gomes, R. C. (2006). Stakeholder management in the local government decision-making area: Evidences from a triangulation study with the english local government. *Brazilian Administration Review, 3*(1), 46–63.

Government of Romania. (2018). *Open government partnership. National Action Plan 2018-2020*. Retrieved from: http://ogp.gov.ro/nou/wp-content/uploads/2018/11/Romania-2018-2020_NAP_EN.pdf

Guimarães dos Santos, L. P. (2015). Comparing the use of forward-looking and contemporary performance measurement to formulate incentive contracts in the presence of the horizon problem: An experimental analysis. Universidade Federal da Bahia, Faculdade de Ciências Contábeis, Salvador, BA, Brazil. Retrieved February 4, 2019 from https://www.scielo.br/pdf/rcf/v26n68/1519-7077-rcf-201501060.pdf

Heinelt, H., & Magnier, A. (2018). Analyzing governance through local leaders' perceptions: Comparative surveys, academic networks and main results. *Revista Espanola de Ciencia Politica, 46*, 151–172.

Heinelt, H., Magnier, A., Cabria, M., & Reynaert, H. (Eds.) (2018). *Political leaders and changing local democracy the European mayor*. Palgrave Macmillan.

Hood, C. (1995). The new public management in the 1980s: Variation on a theme. *Accounting Organizations and Society, 20*(2–3), 93–109.

Hou, Y., Moynihan, D., & Ingraham, P. W. (2003). Capacity, management and performance: Exploring the links. *American Review of Public Administration, 33*(3), 295–315.
Hughes, O. (2003). The traditional model of public administration and public management. In *Public management and administration*. New York: Palgrave, Macmillan.
Hustedt, T., Randma-Liiv, T., & Savi, R. (2020). Public administration and disciplines. In G. Bouckaert & W. Jann *European perspectives for public administration: The way forward*. Leuven University Press. Project MUSE. https://doi.org/10.1353/book.72918
Kelman, S. (2007). Public administration and organization studies. *Academy of Management Annals, 5*(1), 225–267.
Kyriacou, A., & Roca-Sagalés, O. (2018). Decentralization and governance in Europe: Evidence from different expenditure components, EN - Governance and Economics research Network. Retrieved February 7, 2019 from http://infogen.webs.uvigo.es/WP/WP1802.pdf
Ladner, A., Keuffer, N., & Baldersheim, H. (2015). Self-rule index for local authorities (Release 1.0). Final report Tender No 2014CE16BAT031. Retrieved February 8, 2019 from https://ec.europa.eu/regional_policy/sources/docgener/studies/pdf/self_rule_index_en.pdf
Lane, P. J., Cannella, A. A., & Lubatkin, M. H. (1998). Agency problems as antecedents to unrelated mergers and diversification: Amihud and Lev reconsidered. *Strategic Management Journal, 19*, 555–578.
Lane, J.-E. (2013). The principal-agent approach to politics: Policy implementation and public policy-making. *Open Journal of Political Science, 3*(2), 85–89.
Leruth, L., & Paul, E. (2006). A principal-agent theory approach to public expenditure management systems in developing countries. IMF Working Paper, International Monetary Fund.
Lichtenstein, B., Uhl-Bien, M., Marion, R., Seers, A., & Orton, J. D. (2006). Complexity leadership theory: An interactive perspective on leading in complex adaptive systems. *Emergence: Complexity and Organization, 8*(4), 2–12.
Marion, R. (1999). Resource dependency: The emergence of order. In R. Marion (Ed.), *The edge of organization: Chaos and complexity theories of former social systems*. Thousand Oaks: Sage.
Marin, M. (2015). *Absorption of European funds for the communes of Romania: The role of administrative capacity* (Absorbţia fondurilor europene pentru comunele din România: rolul capacităţii administrative). Iaşi: Editura Lumen. https://bibliotecadesociologie.ro/en/download/marin-monica-2015-absorbtia-fondurilor-europene-pentru-comunele-din-romania-iasi-lumen/
Marin, M. (2016). City halls and competition for European funds: The case of "white spots". (Primăriile şi competiţia fondurilor europene: Cazul "punctelor albe"). *Sociologie Românească, 14*(02–03), 35–49.
Marin, M. (2020). Determinants of the absorption capacity of EU funds for the rural municipalities of Romania. *Romanian Statistical Review, 1*, 3–21. Retrieved June 7, 2020 from http://www.revistadestatistica.ro/wp-content/uploads/2020/03/RRS1_2020_A1.pdf
Marteau, J.-F., Czapski, R., Ionescu-Heroiu, M., Burduja, S. I., Nunez, A. B., Cristea, M., Moldovan, S. C., Rusu, R., Man, T.-C., Rizescu, A., Gaman, F., Luca, O., Stanescu, A. A., Todor, C. D., Tulea, M., Armasu, A., Florea, C., Postolache, G. C., & Iliescu, M. (2014). Improved prioritization criteria for PNDL projects (English). In. Washington, D.C.: World Bank Group. Retrieved February 8, 2019 from http://documents.worldbank.org/curated/en/333081467993173873/Improved-prioritization-criteria-for-PNDL-projects
Ministry of Health. (2016). Regional health plans. Published in the Official Gazette no. 988 bis from December 8, 2016.
Ministry of Labor, Family, Social Protection and Elderly. (2015). National strategy on social inclusion and poverty reduction 2015–2020 Romania. Retrieved http://www.mmuncii.ro/j33/images/Documente/Familie/2016/StrategyVol1EN_web.pdf
Ministry of Regional Development and Public Administration (MDRAP). (2018). Report on the territorial status in Romania 2017 (Raport privind starea teritoriului Romania 2017). Retrieved February 8, 2019 from http://www.mdrap.ro/userfiles/Raport%20privind%20starea%20teritoriului%202017.pdf

Mures County Council. (2012). Territorial development infrastructure strategy for Mures county, transport infrastructure. Strategy synthesis. Retrieved February 1, 2019 from http://www.cjmures.ro:1880/urbanism/patj/parte_scrisa/Partea%20III%20vol%20XI%20-%20Strategia.pdf

O'Toole, L., Jr., & Meier, K. (2010). In defense of bureaucracy. *Public Management Review, 12*(3), 341–361.

Pfeffer, J., & Salancik, G. [1978] (2000). Design and management of resource-dependent organizations (Proiectarea şi managementul organizaţiilor dependente de resurse). In M. Vlasceanu (Ed.), *Organizational theory. Collection of texts* (pp. 57–66). Faculty of Political Sciences. National School of Political and Administrative Studies.

Pfeffer, J., & Salancik, G. [1978] (2003). *The external control of organizations*. Stanford: Stanford University Press.

Popescu-Criveanu, S., Popescu-Criveanu, I., & Petrescu, A. M. (2014). Romania's territorial development strategy. Background Studies. Study no. 15. Localities' network according to their rank and importance. Beneficiary: Ministry of Regional Development and Public Administration. Retrieved February 1, 2019 from http://sdtr.ro/upload/STUDII/15.%20Sinteza_Reteaua%20de%20localitati%20dupa%20rang%20si%20importanta.pdf

Prefect's Institution. (2017). Report on implementing the objectives from the economic and social development program of Satu Mare County in the first 9 months of 2017. Retrieved June 16, 2020 from https://sm.prefectura.mai.gov.ro/wp-content/uploads/sites/32/2017/12/Realizari-9-luni-ultim-doc.compressed.pdf

Romanian Court of Accounts. (2015). Audit report of performance for the national program of local development funded by the state budget through MDRAP and implemented by local authorities. Retrieved August 31, 2020 from https://www.usr.ro/wp-content/uploads/2017/04/Raport-CC-PNDL-2014.pdf

Salazar Dominguez, J. (2010). *The political determinants of resource allocation in Mexican municipalities. The fund for municipal social infrastructure*. Ph.D. Thesis. Institute of Development Studies. Brighton: University of Sussex.

Scott, W. R. (2004). *Institutions and organizations (instituţii şi organizaţii)*. Iaşi: Polirom.

Sharfman, M., & Dean, J. (1991). Conceptualizing and measuring the organizational environment: a multidimensional approach. *Journal of Management, 17*(4), 681–700.

Smith, R. W., & Bertozzi, M. (1988). Principals and agents: An explanatory model for public budgeting. *Journal of Public Budgeting, Accounting and Financial Management, 10*(3), 325–353.

Swianiewicz, P. (2014). An empirical typology of local government systems in Eastern Europe. *Local Government Studies, 40*(2), 292–311. https://doi.org/10.1080/03003930.2013.807807. Retrieved May 2, 2019 from https://www.researchgate.net/publication/263249742_An_Empirical_Typology_of_Local_Government_Systems_in_Eastern_Europe

Swianiewicz, P., Gendzwill, A., & Zardi, A. (2017). Territorial reforms in Europe: Does size matter? Territorial Amalgamation Toolkit. Centre of Expertise for Local Government Reform, Council of Europe. Retrieved February 3, 2019 from https://rm.coe.int/territorial-reforms-in-europe-does-size-matter-territorial-amalgamatio/168076cf16

Teşliuc, E., Grigoraş, V., & Stănculescu, M. S. (Eds.) (2016). *The atlas of rural marginalized areas and of local human development in Romania*. Bucharest: World Bank. Retrieved February 4, 2019 from https://openknowledge.worldbank.org/handle/10986/24770

Thijs, N., Hammerschmid, G., & Stamule, T. (Eds.). (2018a). Public administration characteristics and performance in the EU 28: Romania. Luxembourg: Publications Office of the European Union. Retrieved February 3, 2020 from https://publications.europa.eu/en/publication-detail/-/publication/90311e18-95fe-11e8-8bc1-01aa75ed71a1/language-en/format-PDF/source-search

Thijs, N., Hammerschmid, G., & Palaric, E. (2018b). A comparative overview of public administration characteristics and performance in EU 28. Retrieved February 3, 2020 from https://publications.europa.eu/en/publication-detail/-/publication/3e89d981-48fc-11e8-be1d-01aa75ed71a1/language-en

Vesely, A. (2013). Accountability in central and Eastern Europe: Concept and reality. *International Review of Administrative Sciences, 79*(2), 310 – 330.

World Bank. (2015). *Alba Iulia: Project prioritization for 2014–2020* (English). Alba Iulia Project Prioritization Washington, D.C.: World Bank Group. Retrieved April 7, 2020 from http://documents.worldbank.org/curated/en/527401468190739988/Alba-Iulia-project-prioritization-for-2014-2020

World Bank. (2018a). *County Partnership Framework for the period FY19-FY23*. Retrieved April 7, 2020 from https://documents.worldbank.org/curated/en/954721529638270108/Romania-Country-partnership-framework-for-the-period-FY19-FY23

World Bank. (2018b). *Romania water diagnostic report. Moving toward EU compliance, inclusion, and water security*. Retrieved April 7, 2020 from http://documents.worldbank.org/curated/en/114311530025860150/pdf/127630-REVISED-W18010.pdf

The manufacturer's authorised representative in the EU is Springer Nature Customer Service Centre GmbH, Europaplatz 3, 69115 Heidelberg, Germany. If you have any concerns regarding our products, please contact ProductSafety@springernature.com

Printed and bound by CPI Group (UK) Ltd, Croydon, CR0 4YY
30/09/2026
02225307-0009